An Eye on the Sparrow

With love

Sally Roth

An Eye on the Sparrow
The Bird Lover's Bible

Sally Roth

Illustrations by Heather Dieter Bartmann

HAPPY CRAB PUBLISHING

Published by Happy Crab Corp., P.O. Box 1329, Laporte, CO 80535, a not-for-profit corporation.

Printed in the United States of America.

Editor: Matt Bartmann
Art Director: Matt Bartmann
Book Design: Sally Roth & Matt Bartmann
Cover Design: Matt Bartmann
Cover Painting, "Home Grown," by Heather Dieter Bartmann
Copy Editors: Sally Roth & Matt Bartmann
Dog Support Team: Dixie & Koko
Cat Entertainment Supplied by: Kitty Ohtwo ("02")
Sally's website: www.sallyroth.com
Contact Sally & Matt at sparrow@sallyroth.com

ABOUT THE COVER
"Home Grown" by Heather Dieter Bartmann

We had a bumper crop of house sparrows this year. Several nest boxes were full, and a few pairs made homes in the barn rafters. All this activity brought visits from kestrels and sharp-shinned and Cooper's hawks. The tangle of grape vines provided a safe haven for the wary. —*Heather Dieter Bartmann*

For information about purchasing a print, please visit www.heatherbartmann.com

⁷ But ask now the beasts, and they shall teach thee; and the fowls of the air, and they shall tell thee:

⁸ Or speak to the earth, and it shall teach thee: and the fishes of the sea shall declare unto thee.

—Job 12:7-8

Table of Contents

Thank you

[5] *...Which of you shall have a friend, and shall go unto him at midnight, and say unto him, Friend, lend me three loaves;*

—Luke 11:5

Three loaves of bread? We asked for a lot more than that.

This book has been a labor of love. Family and friends, old and new, all helped bring this book to life, generously and selflessly. It's been a joint effort, start to finish. And a very personal one.

Thank you, Heather Dieter Bartmann, for the beautiful artwork that graces these pages. You've brought the birds to life, putting in personality with every stroke of your pencils. It means so much to have you and your love for nature be a big part of this book.

Thank you, Tom Wilson, Bill Dieter, and Bonny Dieter, for helping us brainstorm right from the very beginning, and for offering not only endless support, but also great practical ideas. And for sharing the pleasure of your feeder full of house sparrows, your lush green indoor plants in the depths of winter, and your warm sweet cinnamon buns—not necessarily in that order.

Thank you, Lou Bartmann, for dusting off your incredible calligraphy skills and giving these pages even more beauty with your lettering. "Just use a calligraphy font," as some suggested? No way, not when we can have handmade. Handmade with love, even better. Thanks for knowing us so well, too, and keeping those pens out until every last bit was finished.

Thank you, Lila Bartmann, for gently reminding us that flowers were blooming, and real live birds were at the feeder, and music was going on, and good food and friends were ready when we were. What a knack for knowing when we needed a break! Thank you for making it easy to reconnect with real life when we most needed a respite. Thanks, too, for your keen editing eye.

Thank you, Dan Bartmann, for playing devil's advocate whenever we needed a sounding board to kick ideas around. You'd probably argue this (as usual), but your insight and intelligence helped us find our way to the right answer so many times. And kept us laughing.

Thank you, Wes Hammond, for being such a good friend, and for your brilliant suggestions throughout this project. Whenever we asked, "Hey, Wes, got any ideas for...?" you always did. And they were good ones. Thanks, too, for your support in letting people know about this book. We're grateful.

And thanks, all of you just mentioned, for sharing your printers, scanners, thumb drives, and all the other stuff we didn't have.

Thank you, Hannah LaRee Burrows and Jenny Heinzen, for managing to capture our true nature in your photos—no easy task when the subjects tend to cringe at the sight of a camera. You managed to make it fun, and to catch us being ourselves. Thank you.

Thank you, Pim Borman, for livening up our days with your beautiful photos, your sense of humor, and your "what is it?" questions. I'll never forget the cold winter morning I got to take a "walk" through a full year of wildflowers, from the first spring beauties to the last asters, thanks to your photo album. Boy, talk about the best kind of diversion—with the world all white outside the window, I was instantly transported to tender green leaves and an unfolding season of bloom. Wonderful.

Thank you, Stacy Tornio, and everyone else at *Birds & Blooms* magazine, for helping us get the word out. Your belief in this project and your practical support, plus every one of the many comments and messages from *Birds & Blooms* readers, sure made us smile and helped give us even more incentive. Thank you.

Thank you, you incredible and generous donors to our Kickstarter fundraising project. You made this book a real possibility in the first place. Thanks to you, we're able to set these birds free, winging their way out into the world. We've loved meeting every one of you. We look forward to keeping in touch. And we look forward to repaying your donation, we hope, so that you can help others make their dreams real, too.

Special thanks to you, Larry Miller, longtime beloved friend, philosopher, musician, and gardener supreme, for reaching deep into your pocket to help us make our Kickstarter goal. Can't wait to create a new garden for you. One that will attract the first ravens in Evansville, maybe?

And of course, thank you, www.Kickstarter.com, for providing a place where regular people like us can raise money to help their dream become real.

A great big thank you to our first "reviewers," who never even knew the book was coming 'til we dropped it in their laps. "Hey, would you mind reading 300 pages and telling us what you think?" Why, sure, you said.

So, thank you, Dave and Laura, Bob and Sylvia, Lila, Ben, Rex and LaVonne, Dan F, Tina and Alan and Carly and Jonathan, Bill and Ursula, Trisha and Ayla, and everyone else, for taking the time from your busy lives to critique our efforts, and for loving us enough to do so. Boy, talk about feeling humbled. Thank you.

Thank you to the selfless people who created Biblos.com and Biblegateway.com, websites of Bible scholarship that are deeply researched, solidly reliable, and open to anyone—for free.

Thank you, Buckhorn Canyon friends, Richard and Karen, Dave and Amy, Ken and Kelsey, Bonnie and Scott, Adam, George and Muggs, Tom and Mary, Seth, Tom and Le, Valerie and Blake, Don, Mike, Ward, Michelle, Lynn and Rich, Dan F, Dan B, Maya, Tim and Betsy, Doretta, John and Betty, Tom H, Jon and Hannah, and, yep, again, Wes, for putting up with our obsession and enthusiasm as we lived and breathed this book. Thank you for being just as excited about our discoveries as we were, even though it was all we could talk about for months. We love you.

Thank you to you, too. Yes, you, the wonderful person who's reading this book. Thank you for being you. So glad you are interested in the world around you, and in birds, and in learning.

Finally, nearest and dearest of all, thank you, Matt, my husband and best friend. I could've never written this book without you, and I don't mean just because of all the hard work you put into it—the research, the editing, the art direction. Nope, it's because, with you, it's been a joint project from the very beginning. This book. And life itself. I love sharing it all with you.

Thank you.

What Was I Thinking?

What was I thinking? Well, that's simple. If a little embarrassing.

I was thinking this was going to be easy.

After all, the idea for this book has been simmering in my brain for, oh, maybe twenty years now.

It all started the day I met "real" quail, in west Texas, on the very first long road trip of my life.

I already knew bobwhites, which were common in eastern Pennsylvania, where I grew up.

But to me, bobwhites were, well, bobwhites.

And these Texas birds were *quail*. Gambel's quail, the first ones I'd ever seen outside of a picture in a book.

I fell in love at first sight, thanks to their goofy bobbing top-knots and the way they scurried about single file among the mesquite. Seemed there was always one laggard, who you could almost hear thinking, "Wait for *meeee!*" as he hurried to catch up.

Yep. I was totally charmed.

That night, in a motel room, looking for something to read, I reached for the Gideon Bible.

It happened to fall open at a story about quail.

Quail that dropped from the night skies to feed the sleeping, starving Israelites, who were on their Exodus.

It was a great story, the kind the Bible is full of—Daniel in the lion's den, David and his slingshot, Noah and his Ark, Joseph's coat of many colors, and on and on.

But, hey—hang on a minute.

Quail don't migrate.

So why was a massive flock crossing the sea? And at night?

When I got home from that trip, I found my big, heavy *Birds of the World* book and tried to figure out what was going on.

Aha.

Our American quail don't migrate. But the common quail of the Old World sure do. By the millions. At night. Right along the edge of the Mediterranean—and often over the water.

I was hooked.

A Seed Waiting to Sprout

Pulling out the King James Bible, I started paging through, looking for references to birds.

Wow! There were all sorts of birds in there!

Ravens. Eagles. Vultures. Storks. Owls. Even a bittern, one of my favorite birds.

And of course, doves. Including maybe the most famous Bible bird of all, Noah's dove.

I made lists. Lists of the birds mentioned in the Bible. Lists of the Scripture references to birds.

Then other projects got in the way, and I set this one aside.

For twenty years.

Oh, it still came to mind every time I saw a bittern. Or a raven. Or a crane. "Should write that book someday," I'd mutter.

Meanwhile, I was writing books about other birds—the ones that visit our feeders or backyards, but don't get a starring role in the Scriptures.

This year, the birds of the Bible came back around.

I was ready.

Ready to write about other birds I love. The big birds. The swamp birds. The sea birds.

And besides—this was gonna be easy!

A cinch to pull it together, I thought. Just talk about today's birds in relation to those ancient ones. And how their natural behavior inspired the Bible quotes.

"Research is already done," I told friends who asked how long it was going to take to write this book.

Yes, I'd long since collected every Bible quote I could find— there are 300 or so—and pulled them together, arranged by type of bird, plus those that just said "birds" in general.

That sure felt like research. Hey, it'd taken days. Okay, maybe a couple of hours per day. But days. Maybe even weeks.

And I'd done more! I'd already spent some time thinking about those verses, about the habits of the birds themselves, and how I would correlate that behavior to the quotes.

Yep, this book would be a cinch to write.

Haha. Little did I know.

Somebody Say "Learning Experience"?

Once I actually dug in, the truth of how much I needed to learn was overwhelming.

I couldn't write about doves, for instance, without learning about the doves of the Middle East. Where I've never been.

Even familiar birds needed deeper knowledge than I had stored in my brain. How fast does a golden eagle fly? How wide are those wings, anyhow?

And that was the easy part.

I'm not a Bible scholar. Nor am I a Christian. So I had to learn, or relearn, the whole story behind every one of those verses. What was going on when God sent the rain of quail? Who were the Israelites? How far were they going?

I'm not much good at geography, either. If a bird's current range is Iraq, would that have included the Kingdom of Judah? Where was Edom? Is the Lebanon of today the Lebanon of two thousand years ago? And exactly where is the Great Rift Valley?

Eventually, every single question was answered.

But I didn't do it alone.

I could've never written this book without the help of my husband, Matt.

We dove into it together, researching for 8, 10, 12 hours straight, day after day, week after week. Totally absorbed in learning, which for us is just plain fun.

"How can it be getting dark already?"

"Did we eat anything yet?"

"Boy, is my back stiff...."

This was detective work. And we both love trying to solve a good mystery.

Not a Single Missing Piece

While our real-life bird friends came and went at the feeder outside the window, we searched for the answers to our many questions. It felt like we were working on a 5,000-piece jigsaw puzzle. With many a "Eureka!" moment, as each small piece slipped into place.

"Did you know...?"

"Cool! Did you know...?"

You should've heard me holler when we finally worked out exactly which species of dove it was that Noah released from the Ark. I felt like we'd won the Nobel Prize.

Finally, every last piece of the puzzle was in place. Not by trying to wedge them in—"It looks like it should go here... *grunt*"— but by researching until every bit slid neatly into place.

A pleasure, for sure, to put all the pieces together.

But "easy"?

What was I thinking?

What They Are Thinking

"Hey, would you mind reading 300 pages and telling us what you think?"

Okay. We tried. Tried to get former President Jimmy and Rosalynn Carter to write this section—their Mideast ties seemed a natural fit, and we'd learned they're both big bird lovers.

But seems "because of the large volume of manuscripts they receive and requests for book endorsements, as a policy, they decline such requests."

Fine.

So we went with "regular" people instead. Poor unsuspecting acquaintances of all persuasions—religious, not religious, bird lovers and non-bird lovers alike—onto whom we dropped the book and asked for unvarnished opinions.

Almost every reply we got started with, "This wasn't what I was expecting."

And then they had other things to say. We weren't fishing for praise. But we love that everyone got the point: This is a bird book.

Jimmy and Rosalynn couldn't have said it better.

Truth and Joy

There are so many ways of reading Scripture, and Sally Roth's is a new one. In all her books, Sally has always taught us to look afresh at the things we take for granted, and find the truth, pleasure, and joy in the world around us. She has done it again. —*Ben*

A New Look

This book causes you to look at the Bible in a new way, bringing into light small details that I can almost guarantee no one would have picked up on previously. A great read, not just for people who enjoy birds and want to learn more about them, but for people who are looking for a new way to interact with the Bible. —*Lindsay*

Snottygobbles!

I'm not religious in the least, and books about the Bible are not usually on my list. This book is not about the Bible, but about birds mentioned in the Bible, told in Sally's inimical, witty style, but with solid factual accuracy. Enjoy the book and learn about snotty-gobbles and other weird things! —*Pim*

The Birds Around Us

As an Episcopal Christian who has always believed that science and the Bible go hand in hand, I appreciate books that examine the text and discuss the scientifically correct references. Not only did I learn about Biblical references to birds in greater detail, enhancing my understanding of the Scriptures, but I also learned a lot about the birds that surround me in my daily life thousands of years after the Bible was first written. —*Ted*

The Birdwatcher's Bible

Fantastic! It's a birdwatcher's book, but the Biblical part is vital—the explanation of the reasons behind those references is extremely valuable. People wanting to understand the Bible better will find this useful, I know. And ditto for understanding birds. You make it fun and interesting to read about birds. —*Judy*

For Anyone, Religious or Not

I've been looking for a book like this for years, and didn't really know it. This is an excellent complement to the library of anyone, religious or not, who is trying to have a better understanding of the natural world. —*Joe*

An Absolute Delight

Sally Roth is one of the most talented nature writers I've ever had the pleasure of reading. Everything she writes is an absolute delight, and this book is no different. Get ready to be entertained while gaining a whole new knowledge and appreciation of birds.

—*Stacy Tornio, editor of* Birds & Blooms *magazine*

Weaving a Tapestry

"His Eye Is on the Sparrow" is one of my favorite hymns. In my spiritual wanderings, from Catholicism through Buddhism and just about everything in between, I have retained my love of Scripture. The manner in which Sally weaves the scriptural quotes into her tapestry of bird lore and fact is nothing short of brilliant.

I am new to bird watching, but have become quickly ensnared by these amazing creatures. *An Eye on the Sparrow* will become, to me, my bird bible. I highly recommend it to one and all. —*Keena*

What, No Parrots?

As a bird formerly worshiped by Egyptians, I am disgusted at the lack of references made to me in the Bible and in this book. Who do they think they are, walking right through my land and failing to note my superiority? —*Isis, the African Grey*

Author's note: Sorry, Isis. Maybe we'll tackle hieroglyphics next time.-SR

Hmmm...

My first thought was, "The Bible and birds, hmmm?" I have not been drawn to teachings of the Bible, but I have been drawn to birds. Birds have taught me the rhythm and pulse of the planet, of the seasons, of life, and at times, of death. Birds have taught me to be still and to wait and to watch. Sally's writing has also taught me to be still and to wait and to watch. She is the muse of our avian friends. She tells it like it is...not all glory, not all gory, just as it is...rhythm and pulse. She moves me to consider world travel to see these winged marvels in their native, historic habitats. —*Lila*

Thought-Provoking

As an American Jew who has wandered parts of the Middle East in search of birds and answers, this book caught my attention right away. It provides a wealth of factual information about the many birds mentioned in the world's most well read history book, the Bible. Truly a thought-provoking read, for not just the bird lover but the science-minded, the religious, the agnostic, the inquisitive...for anyone who is interested in seeing what is not always obvious in the ancient writings of the Bible.

—Tina Newfield, supporter of Arava Institute (www.arava.org),
an environmental organization in the Middle East

Fun to Read

The Bible might be our very best source for insight into how humans and birds interacted through history. This book is fun to read...a rich resource for understanding our language and literature, and the interdependence of people and wild creatures. *—Rick*

Making Connections

Examining the life and habits of the actual birds in the Scriptures gives even greater meaning to the message. I'm glad someone took the time to make the connection for me—it is a delightful and meaningful read! Write more! *—Richard*

Author's note: Will do, Richard. Thanks! But first, we gotta go travel a bit and talk about this one. And try to mollify Isis the African Grey. –SR

What You Didn't Know

Sally's done it again. Her latest bird book is a treat! Perfect for bird watchers or anyone interested in the Biblical lands; you will be amazed at what you didn't know. Well researched, of course, but I most appreciated how she interspersed the science and history with interesting tidbits, lighthearted humor, firsthand observations, and illustrations. It will be a great gift for friends and family.

—LaVonne Ewing, publisher, PixyJack Press
(www.pixyjackpress.com), and bird watcher

Birds Do Matter

Sally's presence in this book is all over the pages. You can smell the pond muck on her boots and see her crouching behind a handful of weeds. As always, my favorite characters are the brash, unapologetic ones—"just birds being birds," she reminds us. Once Sally shares what's intriguing or even heartbreaking about them, I can never not know how much they matter. —*Laura*

Greater Meaning

As a Christian, lover of wildlife, and teacher of both, I found *An Eye on the Sparrow* entertaining, educational, and even spiritual. One does not need to be steeped in theology to take Sally's journey. She is simply utilizing the stories of the Bible to deliver to us birders a whole new realm of our ever-loved wildlife.

As for us Christians, this read is a lighthearted spiritual tour providing a meaningful understanding of the Bible's use of avian characters.

For those of us who love both God and His wildlife, Sally's art transcends to an essential aid for our own deeper connection with each and will become a quintessential tool for sharing these passions with our children. A Must Read for all.

> —*Peter W. Hurley, one of God's children and the owner of Hurley-Byrd Wildlife Feeders (www.hurleybyrd.com)*

And now it's your turn (Jimmy and Rosalynn, you reading this??). What do you think? Good, bad, or in between, we'd love to know. (Well, as long as you're not an irritated African Grey parrot, that is.) Stop in at www.sallyroth.com, join the "Come On In, Let's Talk" forum, and let's talk. Or if you'd rather email, just drop us a note at sparrow@sallyroth.com.

We look forward to hearing from you!

> —*Sally & Matt*

Chapter 1

A Mixed Flock

Just Passing Through

> [20] *And God said, Let the waters bring forth abundantly the moving creature that hath life, and fowl that may fly above the earth in the open firmament of heaven.*
>
> —Genesis 1:20

Very few birds are mentioned by name in the Bible, although the area is home to hundreds of different species.

Those that do get called by name are special. They have habits that could be used as an analogy, a metaphor, a virtue, or a warning—a symbol that readers of the verses would understand.

So, sure, eagles come winging in, called by name in a lot of verses. Doves get a starring role in the Scriptures. Storks and cranes are worthy of special notice. So are vultures and hawks.

Ravens and owls? You bet. Quail may be small, but they serve a mighty purpose. Sparrows? Just as vital.

Even the oddball bittern carries a lot of weight.

You can read about these birds—the stars and the best supporting actors—in other chapters in this book.

But to me, every bird is special.

So I noticed the dearth of bird names right way.

Why didn't the prophets see wrens in their visions? Or night-ingales? Or bee-eaters? No sandpipers, with all those mud flats?

I guess the writers had other things on their minds. And giving recognition to specific birds was way at the bottom of the list. Besides, lots of Bible verses refer to birds (or fowls) in general, so they may have decided that a one-size-fits-all word covered the rest.

Still, a handful of other species do make it into the pages of the Bible by name.

Most rate only a brief mention or two. A cameo appearance.

But, since coming across an actual bird name in Scripture—birds other than the stars, that is—is such a relatively rare occurrence, let's look at them one by one.

Swallows

> [2] As the bird by wandering, as the swallow by flying, so the
> curse causeless shall not come.
>
> —Proverbs 26:2

Remember the comic strip "Goofus and Gallant" in *Highlights for Children* magazine? I used to love reading that magazine at the dentist's office when I was young. But I never could stand Gallant. He was a good kid, for sure. But a little too good. Perfect, in fact.

Goofus seemed more like me, making one mistake after another. Not maliciously, of course, or maybe I've just given him more credit than he deserves, thanks to my dim memory of those stories.

The Book of Proverbs is a lot like Goofus and Gallant. But it's way better at getting across a lesson than that heavy-handed comic strip.

Each verse is a self-contained lesson in wisdom. The wise way is contrasted with a fool's way, so that the reader can instantly get the point of the lesson.

Or maybe not instantly, in the case of Proverbs 26:2. The old-fashioned language makes us pause a bit to puzzle it out.

A "curse causeless"? A curse that is without cause: It's undeserved.

An undeserved curse never arrives. Because it wanders as the bird, and flies like a swallow.

Now we're talking.

Swallows don't fly in a straight line.

Watch a flock of swallows catching insects over a lake, and you'll see it's like watching swirling snowflakes. Each bird wheels and dives and climbs, weaving in and out of the others without missing a beat.

So, rest easy. The affliction of that curse is never going to get to you. It's flying like a swallow.

And as long as we're in Proverbs 26, let's skip down to another of my favorites, although birds have nothing to do with it.

> [11] *As a dog returneth to his vomit, so a fool returneth to his folly.*

> —Proverbs 26:11

Now that one, we get right away.

Make Yourself at Home

> [3] *Yea, the sparrow hath found an house, and the swallow a nest for herself, where she may lay her young, even thine altars, O Lord of hosts, my King, and my God.*

> —Psalms 84:3

Yea, er, yay, indeed! Hosting a pair of swallows is a delightful experience. The parents are dedicated to their family, and their graceful, agile comings and goings with food for the nestlings are a visual treat for us, too.

Swallows swoop through summer skies both near and far from water, but when it comes time to raise a family, they seek a spot near abundant insects—those that hatch in multitudes from the surface of a stream, lake, or other body of water.

If you live within easy swallow-flying distance to water, say, about a quarter mile, put up a nest box for tree swallows or violet-green swallows.

And if you're lucky enough to have a shed or barn, especially with livestock or chickens—which attract insects, which attract birds—you may be honored with barn swallows that come to plaster their mud cup nests under its eaves. Great insect control, as well as fun to watch.

Feathering the Nest

No matter what sort of basic building materials—mud, straw, grass—a pair of swallows uses as the foundation of their nest, feathers are always a prized commodity.

The birds poke them among the other materials and line the inside of the nest with them to make a soft, well-insulated home.

Feathers can be hard to find in the wild, and that's where we come in. Next time you visit a duck pond, or stop to buy some farm-raised chicken eggs, gather a handful of feathers. Soft, curled breast feathers, especially white ones, are the top prize for swallows.

If you have swallows showing interest in a bird house, a barn, or a hole in your tree, scatter the feathers on your lawn or other open area. In just a short time, every last one will be eagerly snatched up and added to the nest.

Let the swooping begin.

What's All This Chatter?

> ¹⁴ *Like a crane or a swallow, so did I chatter: I did mourn as a dove: mine eyes fail with looking upward: O Lord, I am oppressed; undertake for me.*
>
> —Isaiah 38:14

When I noticed the purple martin house in the yard next door to the home I'd just moved into, I was thrilled.

Then the big, elegant swallows came back from migration, and I learned that they twittered constantly. Loudly. Beginning pre-dawn. And right outside my often-open bedroom window.

Eventually, I learned to sleep through the chatter, which was when I really began to appreciate the martins.

Whenever you're near swallows of any kind, you'll hear constant chirps, chitters, and other vocalizations.

The birds can't help but to burst forth in song, it seems, whether they're on the wing or at home.

And these are sociable birds—they pal around together in flocks, nest in colonies, and roost together at night when they're not tending babies.

Migration is an ever-growing spectacle, as flock after flock joins the group as they make the journey. Look for the travelers perched on power lines. Then get as close as you can, without scaring them, and listen.

Chatter. Sweet, tinkling voices that never take a rest, until the very instant it's time to take off again.

Cormorant

> [11] *But the cormorant and the bittern shall possess it; the owl also and the raven shall dwell in it: and he shall stretch out upon it the line of confusion, and the stones of emptiness.*
>
> —Isaiah 34:11

Isaiah the Prophet is describing his vision of the vast wasteland after the destruction of Babylon. Yep, this was definitely going to be a no-man's land, once God swept it clean.

Only the birds of isolated places would dare to make their homes there. Which just goes to show how uninviting it was going to be to people.

Just one quibble with this verse: It's not only one cormorant who's going to be there. It's a horde. Cormorants nest in colonies, cramming together nearly side by side.

Along the seacoasts where many of these birds live, they usually choose a good-sized flat spot on a rocky cliff or a big rock in the sea. We're talking *big* rocks. Called "sea stacks," these rocks are more like small islands that can protrude hundreds of feet above the surf.

You don't want to get anywhere near a cormorant breeding colony, and Isaiah knew it. The stench carries a long way when the wind is right, and up close, it's enough to make you gag.

Every inch of rock is splashed white with excrement from these fish-eating birds and their babies.

And regurgitated fish is the food that's shoved down throats a million times a day.

Yeah. If the bittern, owls, and ravens weren't enough to keep you away from that place, the thought of nesting cormorants would turn you back in no time flat.

> [14] *And flocks shall lie down in the midst of her, all the beasts of*
> *the nations: both the cormorant and the bittern shall lodge in*
> *the upper lintels of it; their voice shall sing in the windows;*
> *desolation shall be in the thresholds: for he shall uncover the*
> *cedar work.*
>
> —Zephaniah 2:14

As we now know, cormorants nest in colonies. The cities that were soon to be destroyed were big ones, with thousands of buildings set in close proximity.

Hmm. Lots of stone ruins? With horizontal lintels at a good height, to support eggs and youngsters?

Not an unreasonable facsimile of a natural nesting place.

Cormorants just might sign the lease.

And we'll stay away, thanks. Far away.

Riding the Waves

Cormorants are often called seabirds, but their habits are different from those of true ocean-going birds like the albatross or murre, which only come to land at nesting season.

Although you will frequently see cormorants riding the waves of the Atlantic, Pacific, or Gulf of Mexico, or making a dive from the water's surface, they don't always stick to the ocean.

The mostly black birds—there are more than 40 species worldwide—do frequent saltwater coasts. But they also hang out on freshwater lakes and even rivers.

When their bellies are full, cormorants usually leave the water to perch and dry their wings. At night, too, they may seek a roosting place away from the water, often in nearby trees that can accommodate a big bunch of birds. Unfortunately, the excrement of a regularly gathered flock can kill those very trees, as the acidic guano piles up and gets absorbed by the roots.

Pelican

⁶ I am like a pelican of the wilderness: I am an owl of the desert.

—Psalms 102:6

This chapter is a cry of despair, similar to that in the book of Job, in which Job, beset by bad things, calls himself a "companion to owls." Like Job, the Psalmist is feeling forsaken and alone. To make his point, he pulls up the image of two birds of lonesome places.

One difference between the owl and pelican: The owl may be perfectly at home in the dry-as-dust desert. The pelican, on the other hand, belongs at water.

The wilderness is no place for this big fish-eating bird, who can hardly adapt his giant pouched bill to, say, catching a squirrel.

Yet pelicans are sometimes seen in the wilderness. Not in the forest or cruising the cactus, but flying high as they wing their way from one body of water to another on migration, or settled on ponds and lakes.

Pelicans are an ancient bird, but today, most of the species identified from fossils are extinct, and the world is down to only eight living species. And some of those are sinking fast in numbers.

Trouble is, they're just too good at catching fish.

Humans who depend on their own finny catch have resented the competition for centuries, and many pelican populations were decimated in efforts to reduce their effects.

Here in North America, we have two kinds of these fascinating birds to admire: the white pelican, a mostly inland species, and the brown pelican, an ocean-goer.

Both dropped scarily low in numbers in the past, to the extent that the brown pelican was put on the U.S. Endangered Species List. The pesticide DDT was blamed for the decline in brown pelicans; habitat destruction and outright killing affected both species.

Happily, pelicans are now on the rise. In November, 2009, the

Big Gulp

If you could peek into a pelican's pouch, you'd see that it's mostly empty space. The tongue is tiny, almost absurdly so for such a big bird, to keep it from interfering with the pouch's purpose—a fish-catching basket.

The pouch is a remarkable thing, an adaptation of the bird's lower bill, or *mandible*. It's tailor-made for catching a bunch of small fish at one time, after which the pelican squeezes out the water and swallows the catch. And, no, pelicans don't store food in that pouch. Once the catch is drained, it's gulp and go.

brown pelican was removed from the dreaded Endangered list. White pelicans are increasing in numbers, too.

Pelicans of the same species like to hang out together, so you'll often see them flying in a low line over the water or gathered together in what looks like a gossipy group on the shore. They often fish cooperatively, too, with a group of pelicans driving or encircling a school of fish until all of the birds have a chance to feast.

Humans are still competing with pelicans in North America.

As the number of white pelicans—mostly inland birds, nesting as far north as Canada—began to build, those who are passionate about the native trout known as Yellowstone cutthroat sounded an alarm. Seems the birds were eating more than their share in Idaho. The population of pelicans had built to a dozen or more thriving colonies, and of course they chose to live where food—that'd be fish—was abundant.

Unfortunately, those were the same reservoirs and other waterways that attracted residents and tourists hoping for a good catch of Yellowstone cutthroat trout.

Noisemakers and other non-lethal deterrents were tried, but the only surefire way to eliminate the pelican competition was to get rid of the birds. So the state okayed legal culling—that'd be killing—of the big fishing pelicans.

The Idaho Fish and Game Department's five-year plan for pelican control and coexistence ends in 2013, at which point it will likely be re-evaluated. I'm hoping they'll come up with a way for both people and pelicans to enjoy a taste of trout.

Peacock

> [13] Gavest thou the goodly wings unto the peacocks? or wings and feathers unto the ostrich?
>
> —Job 39:13

There's only one mention of peacocks in the entire Bible, and it's right here in Job, the chapter in which God is delineating his many works, humbling the once high-and-mighty Job.

But, "goodly wings"? That's what we're pointing out about peacocks?

Sure, these large fowls have big, powerful wings, which they use to reach high places—trees, rooftops, palace turrets—to roost at night or perch during the day. Most of the time, though, peacocks aren't flying. They're pecking about on the ground hunting seeds and insects, like a flock of spectacular, super-size chickens.

Or, when the mood strikes, they're strutting their stuff and twirling in circles, like the feather-bedecked "Mummers" in Philadelphia's New Year's Day parade.

And peacocks sure have some stuff to strut. That stupendous tail. That breathtaking iridescent cobalt-blue breast. And my favorite ornament—that endearingly silly tuft of tiny feathers atop the head, each wiry shaft crowned with blue.

Males are the gaudy showoffs. The females, or peahens, wear much quieter plumage, with just a low-wattage wash of color here and there.

A Vision to Behold

Not "lucky" enough to live next door to screeching peacocks? Zoos often have a bunch of the birds freely roaming about and showing off those fabulous tail feathers. Visit in spring for the best chance of seeing peacocks compete for female attention by spreading their tails and shrieking at the top of their lungs. Visit in late summer—molting season—for the best chance of finding a dropped feather.

Peacocks as Pets

Peafowl originated in India, Myanmar (Burma), and other Asian homelands. They aren't native to the Bible lands, but they were kept as ornaments by kings and adopted as symbols of royalty.

Peacocks may look exotic, but they're gallinaceous birds, related to chickens and turkeys, and relatively easy to domesticate.

These drop-dead-gorgeous birds are just as popular today as they were back in Bible times. And you don't need to wait until you're invited to the royal palace to enjoy them.

Thanks to their loud, screeching voices, rural folks sometimes keep peafowl as watchdogs as well as pets. The male birds are as fond of crowing as any barnyard rooster—although their decibel rating is way higher. And they're just as protective of their ladies.

Ostrich

[13] *Gavest thou… wings and feathers unto the ostrich?*
—Job 39:13

While we're happy to see the peacock get its due, ostrich wings are really something to brag about. We're talking about a wingspan of 6 feet, and beautiful, to boot. You may recognize those fabulous fluffy plumes from a feather duster, for which they've been used for centuries.

Only one problem with those wings—they're useless for flying.

Ostriches are flightless. The wing feathers lack the tiny barbs that keep other birds' feathers locked together to provide a strong surface for lift and steering.

But those wings are indeed "goodly." The male uses them to impress females during courtship, bowing them in a graceful dance. And both genders employ those big wings to shade their chicks, and themselves, from the searing desert sun. A built-in parasol sure comes in handy in the heat.

Once we get past the wing appreciation in Job, though, it seems the ostrich isn't quite a symbol of virtue. The chapter continues:

> [14] *Which leaveth her eggs in the earth, and warmeth them in dust,*
>
> [15] *And forgetteth that the foot may crush them, or that the wild beast may break them.*
>
> —Job 39:14-15

Yes, these gigantic birds do lay their gigantic eggs in "dust" (sand might be more accurate). And they do cover them to help keep them warm during the cool desert nights and shielded from the sun in the daytime.

Weighing in at 140 to more than 300 pounds, an ostrich's misstep could indeed crush eggs in its own nest. I doubt it's a frequent occurrence, though, because those eggs are tough, often requiring a hammer or a drill to crack the 1/8-inch thick shells. And, of course, the birds are careful. Wild beasts may eat the eggs, though, because those huge protein-packed ovals are a real prize to hungry animals.

But, although the eggs may indeed fall victim to predators, ostriches hardly "forget" the dangers. They're on guard all the time.

A male ostrich keeps a harem, just like deer or elk. To reduce the chances of predation, the male and females guard the nest fiercely, keeping a sharp eye out day and night for any stealthy egg-eaters that may be approaching.

Extreme Athletes

Ostriches look like a conglomeration of mismatched parts, but they're perfectly adapted to desert life. Every inch of the bird serves its purpose.

Deserts or African savannah aren't easy places to live. But ostriches have a great set of physical defenses, and a fierce personality hidden within that silly-looking body.

These are the kick-boxers of the bird world. When cornered, the huge bird kicks forward, delivering a blow that can stun or even kill. Their feet have only two toes, with the outer toe tipped by a strong claw and the inner toe hardened like a hoof. And those strong feet and legs are something to be feared.

So is the running power of an ostrich. Fastest thing on two legs, an ostrich can cover 9 to 16 feet in a single stride. The birds are sprinters that can reach more than 40 mph, and long-distance athletes that can hold a 30-mph pace for miles.

Not to mention that long neck, which provides muscle power and a long reach, should the ostrich suddenly decide to deliver a vicious peck.

Oh, and let's not forget those extra-big eyes: At 2 inches in diameter (ours are only an inch), they're among the largest of any land animal. Consider the bird's great height, coupled with those

giant-sized orbs, and you can see that it's not very easy to escape an ostrich's notice. I sure wouldn't want to be a predator that disturbs the nest and incurs an ostrich's wrath. And, besides, there's not much opportunity, with the caretaking parents close at hand.

In the daytime, the females of the harem take turns incubating the eggs. Their pale feathers blend in perfectly against the dusty desert. With the bird's long neck stretched flat upon the sand, its big lump of a body looks like just another desert rock. At night, the darker male—more suited to camouflage at night—takes over.

Still, predators can outwit or overpower the big birds. So, yes, wild beasts may indeed get the eggs.

Girls' Night

> [16] *She is hardened against her young ones, as though they were not her's: her labour is in vain without fear;*
>
> —Job 39:16

More negativity about ostriches, but easy to refute, once we realize what's going on in ostrich life: Some of those young'uns *aren't* hers.

Ostriches lay their eggs in what ornithologists call a *communal nest*. The "nest" is just a pit that the male bird scrapes out with his strong feet. "Here you go, girls," he says to his harem, which may include as many as seven females.

The dominant female—yep, there's always a top dog—lays her eggs first, followed by the rest of the wives. When everyone's done laying, the top female comes back to cover the nest with dirt.

But first she makes some adjustments. She gets rid of the eggs laid by the weakest females in the bunch, until there are only about 20 eggs in the nest. Yes, she can tell exactly whose egg is whose.

When the eggs hatch, the adults all help rear the chicks, which scoot around in one big group.

It may seem like an odd system, and it's one that's easily misinterpreted. But, for ostriches, it works.

Head in the Sand?

Blame that old folktale on Pliny the Elder (AD 23–79; he died in the eruption of Mount Vesuvius). This Roman naturalist and philosopher wrote *Naturalis Historia* (*Natural History*), an encyclopedia that was touted as encompassing all known knowledge about the natural world.

Fact or fiction? Much of Pliny's book is based on tales he heard from others, not on his personal observations. He seems to have believed every one he heard. And the accounts of exotic animals were often tall tales, which leads to some amusing reading.

When it comes to ostriches, Pliny's masterwork was off the mark, at least as far as intelligence and motive:

"They have the marvelous property of being able to digest every substance without distinction, but their stupidity is no less remarkable; for although the rest of their body is so large, they imagine, when they have thrust their head and neck into a bush, that the whole of their body is concealed."

Ostriches often rest with that long neck stretched out flat, the better for concealing the bird's presence.

As for burying their heads in the sand, ostriches do reach deep to get stones to help them grind their food.

But the birds are hardly trying to block out the world.

They're hyper-aware of their surroundings at all times. As we would be, too, if we had to worry about lions and other meat-eaters trying to sneak up on us.

"I can't see you, so you can't see me"? That's for human kids, not ostriches. These big birds are ready to scramble to their feet at a moment's notice, should a stalking predator come near.

Honorable Mention

> [13] *And these are they which ye shall have in abomination among the fowls; they shall not be eaten, they are an abomination....*
>
> —Leviticus 11:13

Or perhaps not-so-honorable mention, since these are the birds included in the Bible's lists of dietary prohibitions. The "unclean" ones, because they eat flesh or fish or carrion.

Still, it's nice to see some other names, so we can picture what birds we might see should we travel to the Bible lands.

> [17]*And the little owl, and the cormorant, and the great owl*
> [18]*And the swan, and the pelican, and the gier eagle,*
>
> —Leviticus 11:17-18

Why, look, here's our stinky cormorant friend again, keeping company with owls, swans, pelicans, and gier eagles.

Wow! A pelican! Nice to see him again! Except that he's an abomination. But hey, okay, we get the idea.

Why a swan? Other Bible versions turned the Hebrew transliteration *hat·tin·še·met* ("the white") into flamingo, ibis, or white owl. Swans eat plants and grain, but they do occasionally swallow a fish or frog, and that would toss them onto the "unclean" pile of birds.

And the Bible warns us away from other birds as well. Here's the whole of Leviticus 11, which deals with eating birds—or rather, not eating birds. The list is echoed in Deuteronomy 14.

> [13] *And these are they which ye shall have in abomination among the fowls; they shall not be eaten, they are an abomination: the eagle, and the ossifrage, and the ospray,*
> [14] *And the vulture, and the kite after his kind;*
> [15] *Every raven after his kind;*
> [16] *And the owl, and the night hawk, and the cuckow, and the hawk after his kind,*
> [17] *And the little owl, and the cormorant, and the great owl,*

¹⁸ And the swan, and the pelican, and the gier eagle,
¹⁹ And the stork, the heron after her kind, and the lapwing, and the bat.
—Leviticus 11:13-19

Whew. Okay, by my count, that's only 20 species of birds we're not supposed to eat.

Oops, not so fast.

"After his/her kind" means all related birds, so we're talking more like 70 or 80 different kinds that can't go on the table. *All* herons. *All* hawks. And so on.

The good news? None of the "unclean" birds are likely to be found at the grocery store. For thousands of years, most people around the world have followed the same guidelines that are laid out in this section of the Bible.

Reading Between the Lines

See some unfamiliar bird names in those Biblical prohibitions? Here's a handy cheat sheet to use, next time you're making that grocery shopping list:

Ossifrage. The lammergeyer, also known as the bearded vulture.

Night hawk. Not our scimitar-winged common nighthawk (*Chordeiles minor*), but an owl, possibly the barn owl.

Cuckow. Some translators believe this meant a seagull; however, Old World cuckoos do eat flesh (young birds, plucked from nests).

Lapwing. The lapwing is a plover with no "unclean" habits to speak of; like other plovers, it eats mainly insects and invertebrates. Scholars believe this may have meant the hoopoe, the official bird of Israel, which eats mainly insects but also frogs and reptiles.

Bat. Not a "fowl," but it is winged, so this was a handy place to put it in the list of critters.

A MIXED FLOCK
Swallow, Cormorant, Pelican, Peacock, Ostrich

American range: Swallows, across the country; cormorants, also widespread, at bodies of water, salt or fresh; white pelican, coasts and inland; brown pelican, coasts and occasional vagrant inland.

At the feeder: Of this mixed bunch of birds, it's only swallows that may occasionally visit feeders, for crushed eggshells, or to collect proffered white feathers for nests.

American species: 9 species of swallows; 6 species of cormorants; 2 species of pelicans. No ostriches or peacocks running around in the wild here, sorry, unless they escaped from captivity.

Species in the Bible area: 8 species of swallows; 3 species of cormorants; 3 species of pelicans; 1 species of ostrich. Another ostrich of Bible lands, the once very common Mediterranean or Middle Eastern ostrich, is now extinct, as of about 1966.

A note on translation: Various versions of the Bible may differ on exactly which bird is being referred to, but the Hebrew transliterations are unique to the verses that are quoted in this chapter: The swallow, *kə·sūs;* the pelican, *wə·haq·qā·'āṯ* or *liq·'aṯ;* the cormorant, *haš·šā·lāḵ;* and the ostriches, *rə·nā·nîm.*

Chapter 2

Stork Crane Heron
Skinny Legs

[7] *Yea, the stork in the heaven knoweth her appointed times; and
the turtle and the crane and the swallow observe the time of
their coming; but my people know not the judgment of the Lord.*

—Jeremiah 8:7

I love long-legged birds.

Maybe that's because my own legs are short and stumpy.

"Wish I was taller," I often say, stretching on tiptoes to reach a
can on the top shelf of the kitchen cabinet.

"Fine," I grumble, reconciling myself to my limitations and
dragging over a chair to clamber up on.

Or maybe it's because, with legs-up-to-there, I would instantly
be transformed into a lithe, willowy beauty. I'd wear heels, then, to
accentuate my graceful limbs, instead of hiking boots and goofy
but practical Crocs™.

More likely, though, even with my new leggy physique, I'd
still be a gawky klutz.

Watching herons, cranes, and other birds with lengthy legs
helps support that notion.

Because, even with long stems, these birds aren't exactly the picture of grace.

And that's another reason I love them—as they stagger to a landing, or stumble on a takeoff, they remind me of me.

Yep, we're klutzes.

Once these big birds are in the air, though, we have nothing in common. There, the long-legged birds are the picture of elegance.

Neck In? Neck Out?

It's easy to figure out which sort of long-legged bird you're looking at when it's in flight—just look at the neck. Herons fly with their necks tucked back, folded into a tight, rounded S-curve. Storks and cranes fly with their necks out in front; they may curve their necks somewhat, but they don't pull their heads back into their shoulders. Well, except for the marabou stork, which flies with its neck tucked back like a heron. Always one oddball in the family.

On the Wing

> [9] *Then lifted I up mine eyes, and looked, and behold, there came out two women, and the wind was in their wings; for they had wings like the wings of a stork: and they lifted up the ephah ["the basket"] between the earth and heaven.*
>
> —Zechariah 5:9

Unlike birds of prey, which are often only vaguely identified in the Bible, long-legged birds get called by name.

They're storks. Or herons. Or cranes. And in one case, ibis.

These birds all look somewhat alike at first glance—extra-long legs, heavy long bill, big football-shaped body (that's "football" to Americans; "rugby ball" to you folks in other countries).

So when Bible writers wanted to use these birds to highlight various attributes, they went with specific birds, not general "long-leggeds," say.

In the verse from Zechariah, it's flight that gets the attention.

Storks are the long-distance champs among these skinny-legged birds, funneling back and forth over Bible lands by the many thousands on their twice-a-year migrations.

Plus, storks are really striking in the air.

They soar and glide, usually without flapping, with wings held wide—all the better for admiring their eyecatching black and white coloring.

That's the only color scheme for storks.

Some are black above, white below; others reverse the colors. Many have wings that are painted with the opposite color, for even greater beauty in the air.

And storks are big. Very big.

A few seabirds, including the wandering albatross and the great white pelican, outdo the largest stork—the marabou—in size.

But among land birds, this massive creature has only one rival for the title of biggest bird. The Andean condor of South America wins the bragging rights for wingspan. But only by a few inches.

And not always—"average size" is used for the comparison. Some individual birds, of both species, have wings that are slightly longer than average, or slightly shorter.

May as well call it a tie.

Feather Boa

Hats were all the rage in the Gay Nineties—1890s, that is—and the more outlandish, the better. Birds died by the millions to provide finishing touches on millinery, and marabou storks were among them.

Feather boas were a popular accessory then, too. Wrapped around the neck, the feathery scarves added a flirty touch to the heavy dresses of the day, as Henri Toulouse-Lautrec immortalized in "Woman with a Black Boa."

The fad for feathers continued right through the Roaring Twenties. Although styles changed, fluffy marabou was still in vogue. Dangle a boa, decorate your cloche, put a puff at your neckline—for a flapper, all good fun.

Not much fun for marabou storks, though. The marabou is a massive bird. It stands 5 feet tall, weighs 20 pounds, and has wings that stretch more than 10 feet across, in average specimens.

Since no stork would stand still to have its feathers pulled out, collecting the plumage required killing the birds. As you might expect, that soon led to a decline in marabou storks.

Today, you can still buy "marabou" boas, as well as "marabou" feathers for making fly-fishing lures.

They may be labeled marabou, but they're not stork feathers.

They're from turkeys. Or, in some cases, chickens.

Marabou storks are now protected by international law, and wildlife inspectors make sure no bits and pieces enter the trade to get wrapped around our necks.

Storks at Home

⁷ Yea, the stork in the heaven knoweth her appointed times; and the turtle and the crane and the swallow observe the time of their coming; but my people know not the judgment of the Lord.

—Jeremiah 8:7

Watching birds quickly gives us a feel for the seasons. Oh boy, the robins are back! Must be spring!

In Europe and Asia, where storks are way, way more common than they are in North America, the "appointed time" of these big birds makes them an emblem of springtime.

Some 19 species of storks are found worldwide. Four are common birds of Bible lands, and others pass through on migration.

Storks winter in Africa. But they nest in the north—in Europe, in Scandinavia, in China and Russia, in Israel, Jordan, and Palestine, and in other lands above the Equator.

If you live in stork country, you can't miss their return.

For one thing, they all funnel through the Bible lands, taking advantage of the strip of land between the Mediterranean and Red Sea that's formed by parts of Egypt, Palestine, Israel, and Jordan. They use it as a land bridge between Eurasia and Africa, to avoid flying over great expanses of water.

Hard to miss immense numbers of great big birds flying overhead for a couple of weeks straight.

And just as hard to overlook the homecoming of a stork, because many nest right on the roof of a house or other building. Year after year, the bird returns to its nest, which may be 6 feet across and 10 feet deep, since the storks add to them every year.

Oh sure, you may overlook that first robin of spring when it shows up in your yard.

But a 10- to 20-pound bird scrabbling about on the roof? Even the deepest sleeper in the world will wake up—"Ack! What's that!?"—when a stork comes home.

High Fidelity

A stork couple is monogamous—but the loyalty may last only one nesting season. If the nesting doesn't succeed—if eggs don't hatch into babies, or those babies grow up and fly the coop—the couple may divorce, say researchers who studied white storks.

A stork's fidelity isn't to its partner. It's to the nest.

Those giant constructions, used year after year, are a huge investment in stork time and energy.

So, if the nesting fails, the stork is likely to choose another partner—a different nest—next time around.

It's the male who usually gets the home in the divorce proceedings. How's that go, "Possession is nine-tenths of the law"? Males return first in spring, and they waste no time reclaiming their prized real estate.

By the time females arrive, males are ready to welcome their partners back—or turn a cold shoulder, if last year's brood was unsuccessful.

Females, though, have their own side of the story.

The research showed that, although males may make the decision, more often it's the female who chooses another partner when she returns, if last year's effort was less than a full success.

Bringing Babies

Here's to the stork that brings good babies!

—Wedding toast

Have you ever noticed the logo of the Vlasic® brand of pickles? It's a comical stork, holding a pickle. Moms-to-be are legendary in their craving for pickles. And storks, so we've heard, bring babies.

That pickle craving is based on experience (my own, included). But the connection between storks and babies? Sorry to break it to you, but that's pure fiction.

It's the white stork—that's its name; it's actually white with black wings and tail—who's responsible for the old folktale.

These big birds are the most common, most widespread, and most abundant of the Old World storks.

And they're the birds that nest on rooftops or chimneys.

"Where do babies come from?"

When you're searching for a euphemistic explanation to the inevitable question, it's not a big leap to get to the stork story.

Those giant birds living on your house could easily drop a baby down the chimney. Very believable, to a little kid.

Hans Christian Andersen helped cement the tale, and may have even originated it. In his 1838 story "The Storks," he tells of a stork family on a roof who overhear some boys singing a rhyme in which storks are hung and roasted over a fire.

Never fear, says the mother of the frightened young storks: Not all of the children sang, and the nice ones will be rewarded. *"All parents are glad to have a little child, and children are so pleased with a little brother or sister. Now we will fly to the pond and fetch a little baby for each of the children who did not sing that naughty song...."*

The image of a stork carrying a baby goes back even further, to Greek myth. But here it's baby-stealing, not baby-delivering.

Seems that Greek goddess Hera and a mortal woman named Gerana had some enmity between them, perhaps because Hera was jealous of Gerana's legendary beauty. (You'd think a Greek goddess wouldn't be so insecure—I mean, isn't saying someone "looks like a Greek goddess" a pretty good compliment?)

After Gerana had a baby, Hera turned her nemesis into a stork. Poor Gerana tried and tried to get her baby back, but the people drove the stork away. Did she ever manage to carry off her baby in a kerchief cradle dangling from her beak? We'll never know.

A Single Species

Wood stork status changed from "endangered" to "threatened"

—U.S. Fish & Wildlife Service, December 18, 2012

Poor us. Here in North America, we only get one stork.

It's the wood stork, as boldly patterned as its foreign kin.

Once included on the U.S. Endangered Species List, our wood stork is slowly increasing in numbers these days. It winters only in south Florida, but it nests on a long length of the Gulf and southern Atlantic coasts, as well as in southern California.

And this bird is a wanderer.

When it gets the urge for going, those massive wings carry it far and wide. Sightings have been reported in every state of the mainland, except for Oregon and Washington, and it's been seen in British Columbia and even the Yukon.

Transcontinental Travels

Most American birds that migrate back and forth to Central and South America are small birds—many of them "perching birds," or *passerines,* as they're called. Think orioles, tanagers, wood warblers, vireos, and hundreds of other species that make the twice a year journey.

Many of these species fly long-distance by night, dropping down at dawn to rest and eat. And maybe to thrill us by stopping at our feeders. (Hawks make the journey in the daytime, and you'll find good places to watch that flight in Chapter 8, Falcon & Hawk.)

In Eurasia, it's a little different.

Big birds are on the move in spring and fall. In daylight hours.

Really big birds.

We're talking 6-foot or better wingspans.

And as the flight moves south in fall, gathering birds from all over Europe, Russia, and the rest of that vast continent, millions upon millions of these birds pour across the lands of the Bible as they make their way to Africa.

Smaller birds are moving, too, but it's the big guys that create an awesome spectacle in fall, and again in spring, when they fly north.

Storks. Cranes. Eagles. Giant vultures. Hawks. Falcons. Pelicans.

A living river of wings, filling the sky in incredible numbers.

No one really knows how many birds migrate through the area. Best guess? At least 500 million birds of all descriptions, from Old World warblers to quail to the wide-winged kings of the air. But it could very well be billions.

Israel's Hula Valley, a mile from Syria and Lebanon, and home to the Agamon Hula Preserve in the Galilee panhandle, is one hotspot to watch the big show. But if you happen to be anywhere in the lands of the Bible area when birds are on the move, remember to keep an eye on the sky.

Storks in Trees

¹⁷ *Where the birds make their nests: as for the stork, the fir trees are her house.*

—Psalms 104:17

Some stork species, including our American wood stork, choose the branches of trees, the tops of utility poles, or other stout supports as nest sites. Many species are *colonial nesters,* living in colonies, with each pair having its own great big bowl of sticks. Sort of like suburbanites.

And, just like the storks who build on houses, the birds return year after year to the same homes.

The "fir trees" in this verse are most likely cedars of Lebanon (*Cedrus libani*).

Unlike the conical firs we use for Christmas trees, these graceful cedars have sturdy extra-wide branches, held out horizontally.

Each limb can weigh as much as three tons. Good place to park a giant nest of sticks!

Cedars of Lebanon are long-lived in the extreme—a tree can live as long as a thousand years, if it's not cut down for building ships or temples or other endeavors.

So the happy home would remain for many years to welcome back returning storks.

Our American wood storks also nest in colonies. But they're not very particular about what kind of trees those are.

You'll have to visit the Gulf Coast or southern Atlantic coast, or Florida, to find wood storks at home. And they won't be nesting in cedars of Lebanon, nor on house roofs.

Look for their big, bulky nests in many different types of trees, including bald cypress, mangroves, willows, and even shrubs of the swamps, such as buttonbush.

Whatever's handy, and wherever there's enough room for all their friends, seem to be the guidelines our own storks follow.

Kneejerk Reaction

When our American wood stork wades in water, it keeps its bill submerged to the nostrils and slightly open, ready to snap up anything that swims by. That's mostly fish, but crabs and frogs get snatched, too.

Slowly waving that heavy beak back and forth, the bird reacts like lightning to anything that brushes against its lower mandible.

The response is super fast: twice as quick as a fish's reaction, according to scientists who measure such things.

Why the lower mandible?

Because it gives the stork a much better chance of making the catch. One quick snap of the beak, and there you go.

If it were the upper beak that was tickled, the stork would have to raise its head a bit to snap at the prey. Fraction of a second? Plenty of time for fishie to wave "bye-bye" as it darts out of danger.

Snack Time

> *I once sat and watched them feeding within 20 yards of my blind and was much impressed by the loud clattering of their bills, as they walked about with long, deliberate steps, feeling for their food and scooping it out of the mud and water.*
>
> —A.C. Bent, "The Wood Stork,"
> *Life Histories of North American Birds*

You'd think the naked head of a wood stork would be a big clue as to its eating habits—but it's a red herring.

Although some storks have naked heads, same as many vultures, carrion isn't the main menu item for most species.

Our wood stork, for instance, is a fish eater. Live fish, most of which it finds by touch, not by sight.

Stork eating habits vary somewhat from one species to another. But since all species are wading birds that frequent wet places, fish, frogs, and other aquatic critters are high on the menu.

The white stork, of rooftop fame, eats plenty of meat as well as fish. Small animals and birds go down the hatch with relish.

The massive marabou stork eats carrion, plus living critters of all sorts, even insects.

It often follows vultures to a carcass, letting them do the opening and ripping, and catching pieces tossed aside. And it's common at garbage dumps.

But the marabou stork also has an endearingly fastidious side: It's been observed washing dung beetles—the "scarab" beetle of ancient Egypt, which has the unique habit of rolling balls of excrement—before eating them.

Footballs on Stilts

> [14] *Like a crane or a swallow, so did I chatter: I did mourn as a dove: mine eyes fail with looking upward: O Lord, I am oppressed; undertake for me.*
>
> —Isaiah 38:14

"Cranes!" Wait, that's not quite it. My cry of delight was more like *"CRANES!!!!"*

Once you hear the unearthly rattling, chattering voice of a crane, you'll forever recognize those wild cries that rain down as the birds travel.

And I'd been crane-deprived for a few years, ever since I'd moved from Indiana, where the big gray sandhills gather by the tens of thousands during migration, to the Colorado Rockies.

Now here they were, flying over our very house in the high

mountains. Mere dots we had to squint to see, but those chattering voices were unmistakable.

Definitely time to let out a whoop.

But the cranes that got me so excited weren't whooping cranes.

These guys were sandhill cranes, by far the most abundant American species.

Our whooping cranes, which are slowly climbing back from the brink of extinction, have a different sound. Instead of rattling and chattering like sandhill cranes, they do exactly what their name says, squawking out a single *"Whoop!"* over and over. Imagine the bleating noises of a kid learning to blow a trumpet, and you've got the idea.

Cranes vs. Crops—How About Both?

Used to be, marshes were considered worthless. Couldn't live in 'em, couldn't farm 'em, couldn't build on 'em. Solution? Why, drain them, of course. Yay! No more mosquitoes!

That's what happened to many parts of the vast marshes of the Bible lands. Which meant that millions of cranes and other wetland birds had to change their usual haunts.

But in the past couple of decades, habitat restoration has become a priority in Israel and other places, just as it has in America. We've learned that wetlands can be a good thing, for wildlife and for us.

In Israel's Hula Valley, a prime stopover spot for migrating birds, wetland restoration efforts began in the 1990s. Land that had been drained for farming began attracting thousands of common cranes again, as it returned to marsh.

Oops. Farming is still going on near those restored areas. And it turned out that fields of peanuts were pretty yummy to the cranes.

How to solve the problem of cranes eating crops, without harming the birds? Simple! Put out an even more appealing feeder.

These days, tractors cart wagonloads of corn and other food to the fields, spreading it out to make a "feeder" that's bigger than our typical backyard.

The cranes quickly learned to associate the sound of a tractor with food. Which led to another benefit—tractors now also haul wagonloads of bird lovers to the crane-feeding areas, allowing folks to watch the great birds at close range.

And the cranes have decided to stick around. As of 2013, more than 30,000 of the big gray birds now spend the entire winter in the Hula Valley, instead of moving on to Africa.

That's a lot of bird food. But tourist dollars entirely cover the cost. Cranes and crops can coexist.

On the Move

> *⁷ Yea, the stork in the heaven knoweth her appointed times; and*
> *the turtle and the crane and the swallow observe the time of*
> *their coming; but my people know not the judgment of the Lord.*
>
> —Jeremiah 8:7

Our sandhill crane looks a lot like the most abundant crane of Bible lands, the Eurasian or common crane (*Grus grus*). Both have big gray oval bodies on stilts, with a red patch on their foreheads.

A second species also joins the rattling racket in Bible lands— the Demoiselle crane, who wears a jaunty white tuft of feathers on the back of its head, like a tilted beret.

Both are migrants, like our sandhills and whooping cranes.

As big, noticeable birds that migrate in numbers—not to mention those rattling voices—they join the list of spring harbingers noted in Jeremiah.

Here, too, cranes are a sign of spring. And of fall.

You've got a good chance of spotting sandhill cranes just about anywhere in North America. They nest in the north, and fly south every fall.

The flock that made me holler when they rattled over our home in the Rockies was following a flyway that takes them to a resting spot in southern Colorado and then onward to New Mexico and Arizona. Whatever route they take, cranes gather at stopover sites along the way, congregating in incredible numbers.

Come spring, the birds follow a reverse route to get back to breeding grounds.

The sight, and sound, is enough to make cranes a destination trip. Visit these places during migration to see cranes *en masse*:

- **Bosque Del Apache National Wildlife Refuge,** near the town of San Antonio in south-central New Mexico;
- **Monte Vista National Wildlife Refuge,** in southern Colorado, near Alamosa;

- **Jasper-Pulaski Fish and Wildlife Area** in central Indiana, near Medaryville;
- And for the most mind-blowing spectacle of all? The area around **Kearney, Nebraska,** along the Platte River, where up to 350,000 cranes gather during migration.

Florida Vacation?

It's an odd sight to see sandhill cranes walking about on lawns in towns, suburbs, and other populated areas of Florida, as calmly as if they were giant-sized robins. These Florida sandhill cranes are a subspecies of the wilder birds the rest of the country sees. And yes, they're often backyard birds.

Wade in the Water

> [4] *For an angel went down at a certain season into the pool, and troubled the water: whosoever then first after the troubling of the water stepped in was made whole of whatsoever disease he had.*
>
> —John 5:4

Cranes look a lot like storks and herons, and that resemblance holds true in habits as well as appearance.

Those super-long legs are made for troubling the water.

So, you'll see cranes wading for frogs, fish, and other yummy bites in the shallow water of marshes, lakes, and other wet places.

Like the other birds in this chapter, cranes use their gangly gams to navigate in dry places, too. They often gather in farm fields or grasslands to glean leftover grain, rodents, or insects.

A Happy Trio

Crane families stick together, at least until there's a new nest on the way. In fall, you'll usually see them in groups of three—Mom, Dad, and Junior from that year's nesting.

Even when they're in the midst of an enormous flock at a migration rest stop, the family stays together.

How can you tell who's who?

Youngsters may still beg for food, even at this age. Parents may dance briefly with each other, leaping upward with spread wings.

If behavior doesn't give you enough of a clue, look for the red forehead patch that adult birds wear. It's colored skin, not feathers, and young birds don't get that decoration until they're mature.

Ibis—Or Is It?

> [11] *But the cormorant and the bittern shall possess it; the owl also and the raven shall dwell in it: and he shall stretch out upon it the line of confusion, and the stones of emptiness.*

> —Isaiah 34:11

That's the King James Version of this verse of Scripture, a part of Isaiah's prophecy of the destruction of Judah, and most other translations agree about that owl and raven. But in the Douay-Rheims Bible, it's "the ibis and the raven," not the owl and raven.

Ibises did stalk around in the Bible lands, and they don't mind isolated marshlands at all. In fact, that's where they live.

These are wading birds, like the others in this chapter, and they eat creatures found in water and mud. Their downcurved bills are tailor-made for extracting choice morsels from the mire.

The same difference of opinion in translation occurs in the food-prohibition rules in Deuteronomy and Leviticus. Depending on which version of the Bible you're reading, you may find an ibis in there, too.

Stork on a Spit?

> [19] *And the stork, the heron after her kind, and the lapwing, and the bat.*
>
> —Leviticus 11:19

Yay! Finally, the heron makes its appearance in the Bible. Okay, so it's in a list of unclean birds not to be eaten, but still, it's nice to see one of my favorite birds finally get the spotlight.

We have a handful of heron species in North America, with the most common being the great blue heron, a familiar bird across the country.

Like the other long-leggeds, these guys eat fish, frogs, and other water creatures—and land animals, too, including many voles, mice, gophers, and even small birds.

Often, a quick toss of the prey into the air follows the lightning-quick nab. That ensures the critter goes down the hatch in the right way, instead of possibly getting stuck crosswise.

Open wide, and down goes the still-living prey in one gulp, followed by a few deep swallows to move it through that extra-long neck.

In winter, great blue herons often stalk a productive patch of meadow, farm field, or roadside until the small animals in the grass become hard to find.

If the prey is highly abundant, as when rodents reach a peak in their every-several-years cycle, a loose group of herons may gather to take advantage of the food. Once it's gone, so are the big birds.

STORK, CRANE, & HERON
Various species

American range: Widely distributed across North America; some species have small ranges.

Natural diet: Fish, frogs, and other aquatic creatures, plus small mammals and occasionally nestling birds.

At the feeder: Unlikely to visit feeders, except possibly during extreme weather (droughts, fires, blizzards, and other times of scarce prey). May visit backyards, especially in Southern states, to pick off insects, lizards, and other goodies from plants. Herons may hang out near fishing piers, in hopes of getting a handout.

American species: Wood stork; sandhill and whooping cranes; great blue heron, little blue heron, tricolored heron, great egret, reddish egret, little egret, cattle egret; ibises; roseate spoonbill; and flamingo.

Species in the Bible area: Many, including storks, cranes, ibises, herons and egrets (white herons), Eurasian spoonbill, and flamingo.

A note on translation: The transliterated Hebrew is clear on which bird is which: ḥă·sî·ḏāh, stork; wə·sîs, crane; hā·'ă·nā·p̄āh, heron.

Chapter 3

Bittern

A Brown Recluse

> [23] *I will also make it a possession for the bittern, and pools of water: and I will sweep it with the besom of destruction, saith the Lord of hosts.*
>
> —Isaiah 14:23

What's the strongest possible symbol for a life of solitude, lived in a place of utter desolation?

According to the Bible, it's the bittern.

A fitting symbol of the solitary life, the bittern is one of the most difficult birds to ever get a glimpse of. It dwells in wet, muddy, marshy places, where the going is tough and every splashing, sucking step of a trespasser alerts the secretive bird into retreat.

The bittern of the Bible, and of real life, is a loner. Except for brief encounters at mating season, or when nesting, it eschews even the company of its own kind.

And it's so obsessive about its privacy that it has a whole bag of tricks to prevent it from ever being seen.

Still, it can't hide its distinctive voice.

And that's where to start, when you're trying to track down a bittern—with your ears.

Thunder-Pumper, Stake-Driver, Bog-Pumper

Old-time names for the bittern do a good job of describing the sound it makes. But whatever you call it, the bittern has a voice like no other bird. It sounds almost mechanical, like the rhythmic noise of a pump.

And that's exactly what it is—the bird is pumping air through its throat.

Much like a kid forcing himself to belch, the bittern inhales and exhales big gulps of air to create a loud, booming, rhythmic "song."

Catch a bittern in the act of vocalizing, and you'll see its neck expanding and contracting as if the bird is in convulsions.

The sound carries a long way. And it has an almost ventriloquial quality—it can often be tricky to pinpoint exactly where the sound is coming from.

It's also fun to try to imitate, should you be so inclined. When breeding season hormones are at their height in late spring, you may even trick a male into coming closer to see the odd-sounding competitor that's sounding off. Females generally aren't so easily fooled.

Bitterns of Babylon

> [19] And Babylon, the glory of kingdoms, the beauty of the
> Chaldees' excellency, shall be as when God overthrew Sodom
> and Gomorrah.
>
> —Isaiah 13:19

Babylon sat astride the Tigris and Euphrates rivers, two major channels that flood regularly every spring.

Like the freshwater marshes of the Mississippi River, these Middle East wetlands were perfect habitat for bitterns.

Teeming with fish, frogs, and other good bittern foods.

And inhospitable to people, unless they traveled in small boats or rafts.

And now conditions were going to get even better for bitterns, prophesied Isaiah:

People were going to be erased from the scene.

Great news for bitterns!

The Power of a Symbol

Nearly three quarters of a million words fill the pages of the Bible: 774,746, to be exact, according to scholars' counts of the King James Version.

Yet the bittern is mentioned only three times in the entire book.

Each reference to the bird comes amidst a scene of dreadful retribution from the hand of God.

Total destruction is about to befall the land.

Total, that is, as far as people.

But a very few other living beings will still exist. Including the bittern, which seems to have been called out by name because of the power of its solitary reputation.

Welcome to Desolation Row

> [20] *It shall never be inhabited, neither shall it be dwelt in from generation to generation: neither shall the Arabian pitch tent there; neither shall the shepherds make their fold there.*
>
> —Isaiah 13:20

The bittern is singled out twice in the book of Isaiah. Judah will be destroyed by God, the prophet Isaiah says, and afterward, the way would be clear for the eventual return of the exiled people of Israel.

They'll come home to a land that's been made anew, transformed from a dry wilderness into a homeland that springs alive with "pools of water."

The initial scene, though, is a little less than appealing.

> [21] *But wild beasts of the desert shall lie there; and their houses shall be full of doleful creatures; and owls shall dwell there, and satyrs shall dance there.*
>
> [22] *And the wild beasts of the islands shall cry in their desolate houses, and dragons in their pleasant palaces: and her time is near to come, and her days shall not be prolonged.*
>
> —Isaiah 13:21-22

It's the mighty destruction, and its terrible aftermath. And all those animal and avian symbols of desolation.

> [23] *I will also make it a possession for the bittern, and pools of water: and I will sweep it with the besom of destruction, saith the Lord of hosts.*
>
> —Isaiah 14:23

Don't know much about the habits of satyrs or dragons, so I can't vouch for them.

But I expect that the bitterns who were soon to possess the erstwhile Babylon were saying "Perfect!"

These singular birds like nothing better than living alone among pools of water. Weeping and wailing among the humans, for sure. But for the bitterns—O, happy day!

How Long Can You Hold Your Breath?

> [8] *For it is the day of the Lord's vengeance, and the year of*
> *recompences for the controversy of Zion.*
>
> [9] *And the streams thereof shall be turned into pitch, and the*
> *dust thereof into brimstone, and the land thereof shall become*
> *burning pitch.*
>
> [10] *It shall not be quenched night nor day; the smoke thereof shall*
> *go up for ever: from generation to generation it shall lie waste;*
> *none shall pass through it for ever and ever.*
>
> —Isaiah 34:8-10

Just in case the readers of Isaiah's prophecy didn't get the hint the first time around, the dire consequences to come from the hand of God are spelled out again, 20 chapters later.

Now, this could get a little tricky for bitterns. Burning pitch would cast a heavy pall of smoke over the marsh.

The other birds mentioned could easily fly out of harm's way.

But bitterns only take to the air when it's absolutely necessary. Mostly, they'd be scooting along at ground level among the close-set reeds and rushes, wending their way through the brimstone and the burning pitch.

And the smell of all that brimstone and hot tar could get a little hard to bear.

Fire and Brimstone

Brimstone may sound supernatural, but it's simply sulphur. And while it may reek like rotten eggs, it's also a natural part of life in a marsh.

Sulphur is released into the air all the time in a marsh, in the form of hydrogen sulphide, dimethyl sulphide, and other chemical components.

Raining Fire

Fire is a natural part of life in marshlands. When it doesn't happen as an act of Nature, wildlife managers in the U.S. do prescribed burns. They torch the dry marsh grasses—with petroleum-based accelerants that would create their own tarry smoke—in order to encourage the growth of vegetation more desirable for wildlife.

Burns are ignited every two to four years in salt marshes along the Gulf Coast, and every year in the 27,000-acre Blackwater National Wildlife Refuge (NWR) on the Chesapeake Bay. The frequency of burning depends on conditions, but detailed analysis shows that burning is a good thing for a marsh and for its denizens.

The burns are conducted early in the year—January 1 to March 15 at Blackwater NWR. That's before birds begin nesting. So, the carefully constructed nests that bitterns will later weave into the reeds aren't at risk. Still, birds already in the marsh—including bitterns—would be exposed to the smoke, which at times may be as dense as that from burning pitch.

Maybe not in the wholesale quantities God was talking about in Isaiah 34:9, but little by little, as the muddy sediments are stirred up so that the sulphur compounds can escape.

Then again, recent research shows that a salt marsh can release 1.7 megatonnes of sulphur into the atmosphere—every year.

You may get a whiff of that "brimstone" yourself as your feet sink into the mud in a marsh. The weight of your steps is introducing air into the anaerobic sediments, causing the gases to waft upward onto the wind.

So, the threat of fire and smoke, and the smell of brimstone, would be no strangers in the life of a bittern.

Once again, the bittern who was consigned to that marsh by God saith, "Fine."

Home Sweet Home

> [23] *I will also make it a possession for the bittern, and pools of water: and I will sweep it with the besom of destruction, saith the Lord of hosts.*
>
> —Isaiah 12:23

A life of hermitude sounds totally foreign to most of us. We live surrounded by our own kind, and we enjoy the company. Most of us don't retreat to a cave in the hills or build a shack far off the beaten path.

The isolated life of a bittern? No wonder it's used as a cautionary tale in the Bible.

It's only natural to a bittern, though. Solitude is this bird's preferred way of being.

As for that desolation warned of by Isaiah—a marsh isn't desolate at all, even though we rarely venture into it.

Marshes are brimming with all sorts of life, albeit not of the human kind.

Phragmites Reeds

It was the Assyrian kingdom that aroused such ire in God, its impending destruction foretold by prophets Isaiah and Zephaniah. Its two big cities were Babylon, which nestled in the triangle at the confluence of the Tigris and Euphrates Rivers, and Nineveh, which sat on the east bank of the Tigris across from present-day Iraq.

That area of what once was called Mesopotamia is a floodplain, with the extensive marshes you'd expect, although many acres have been drained. It's one of the ancestral homes of tall, plumy phragmites reeds (*Phragmites australis*). And phragmites marshes are where the great bittern of Eurasia, the bird of the Bible, hangs out.

Phragmites grows around the world. You'll see it in North America, too, its tall plumes covering thousands of acres along coastlines and in smaller marshes. Biologists are still arguing over whether ours is a native subspecies (*Phragmites australis* ssp. *americanus*), probably getting pushed out by the Eurasian species, or whether it's all a single invader. The Eurasian species has the nefarious trick of putting out a toxin so other plants, even closely related subspecies, can't grow nearby.

Our American bittern isn't as fond of phragmites as its foreign relative. You're more likely to find the bird skulking among cattails, or in a mixed growth of native rushes and other marsh vegetation, than you are to find one in a solid patch of phragmites. Still, any thick patch of reeds is worth a look. And a listen.

Humming with Life

Look around you next time you're in a marsh, and you'll notice all sorts of goings-on.

Dragonflies and mosquitoes whine and buzz above the water. A multitude of grasshoppers, ants, and other insects live in the vegetation. Spiders weave their webs from stem to stem or lurk in the grass, ready to pounce.

Small, furry meadow mice or voles scurry among the reeds, and muskrats paddle about in pools and ponds. Northern harrier hawks tilt low over the vegetation, looking to make a meal of them.

Fish, crayfish, and larval forms of insects fill the waters, whether brackish or fresh. Snakes slither about, and lizards and salamanders creep and slide their way over the mud.

And among the stems, red-winged blackbirds, marsh wrens, and a host of other feathered folks sing from the reeds, raise their families, or stop along their migration route to settle for a night's sleep in a safe roost, far from humanity.

As a symbol, a marsh—with nothing but tall grassy plants as far as the eye can see—is a good example of desolation to people.

But it's never devoid of life.

In fact, marshes, or wetlands, as many call them, are among the richest places on earth, as far as living critters are concerned.

Hunting a Hermit

> [11] *But the cormorant and the bittern shall possess it; the owl also and the raven shall dwell in it: and he shall stretch out upon it the line of confusion, and the stones of emptiness.*
>
> —Isaiah 34:11

Stones of emptiness? No problem to a bittern. As long as there's good cover for staying out of sight, and muddy edges to stalk, bitterns are happy.

If you're lucky, you may have a marsh nearby where you can try your own hand at stalking a bittern. Bitterns only live in swampy places, and both saltwater and freshwater habitats suit their habits to a T.

Many National Wildlife Refuges or other nature sanctuaries

include swampy areas, to protect the homelands of specialized birds. Most of those places have hiking trails or even roads traversing the areas, which makes it way easier to gain access and sneak up on the bird.

Even when you find a likely bittern homeland, it's not going to be easy to spot the bird.

And "not easy" is putting it mildly.

You may clearly hear a bittern calling its trademark "pump handle" *unk-a-chunk, unk-a-chunk,* but finding the vocalist with your eyes is a challenge.

It doesn't seem like it should be that hard.

We're talking about a bird with a plump body the size of a large chicken, set on a stout pair of medium-long heron legs with long yellow-toed feet.

Not exactly a needle in a haystack.

Yet the bittern is so sneaky, and so well camouflaged, that trying to zero in on it can drive you to distraction.

In fact, spotting a bittern is so extremely frustrating, and requires so much patience, that you'll probably throw up your hands and give up, long before you see the bird.

On the other hand, you may spot the big brown bird right there in full view, just by happenstance.

Whether you come across a bittern by accident, or whether you spend half an hour standing motionless among swarms of vicious mosquitoes, straining your eyes, once you do see one of these elusive birds, you'll remember it forever.

Did We Say "Sneaky"?

The breast of a bittern is white with vertical brown streaks. Like a tiger, its pattern is perfectly calculated to blend in with the vertical light and shadows of marsh grasses.

Great camouflage, right in itself. But bitterns carry that camouflage to the nth degree.

1. Slowly, slowly, a bittern who knows it's being watched will rotate its body so that its streaky chest faces the observer. The motion is so stealthy that it's almost indiscernible.

2. Meanwhile, the bird ever so gradually stretches its neck and raises its chin until its long, pointed bill is aimed straight for the sky. Nope, no bittern here...just us sharp-tipped blades of marsh grass, thank you.

3. Finally, should the grasses begin to sway at the touch of a gentle breeze, the bittern will undulate, too, keeping perfect time with the waving motion of the vegetation around it. Grasses, or bittern stripes? Almost impossible to tell.

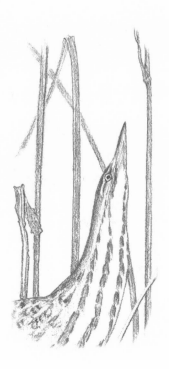

The Dating Game

Bitterns sing on occasion all year round, but it's in spring—courtship time—that they really start *unk-a-chunk*ing left and right, from all over the marsh.

"*Pick me!*"

"*No, me!*"

"*Me! Me! Me!*"

Since the vocalists are hidden among the reeds and rushes, the female bittern has to journey to wherever a possible partner is holding forth. Stepping slowly and carefully among the grasses, she comes closer.

And what a sight she meets. The male does his best love song every few minutes, with a motion that's a little less than romantic: As the bird pumps out its guttural notes, its involuntary jerking motions look just like a bout of forceful vomiting.

Should it be love at first sight—or maybe just, "Yay, I actually managed to find you!"—both birds go into a deep crouch, their backs arched, necks bent back, big bellies low to ground, showing off the white-feathered patches between their shoulders. They slink around, turning their backs on each other, the better to show off their beauty. Ah, love.

Tricks Up Your Sleeve

> [14] ... *both the cormorant and the bittern shall lodge in the upper lintels of it; their voice shall sing in the windows; desolation shall be in the thresholds; for he shall uncover the cedar work.*
>
> —Zephaniah 2:14

Bitterns have a slew of tricks for staying hidden from sight. Counter those with your own clever behavior, and you'll have a good chance of hearing and seeing the Bible's symbol of isolation.

Voracious mosquitoes and biting flies are an irritating plague where bitterns live. Before you begin the hunt, apply insect repellent, or wear a mesh-veil hat, long pants, and a long-sleeved shirt, buttoned up to the neck, so that your involuntary swatting motions don't draw attention. Arm yourself with plenty of patience, too.

Once you're in the marsh:

1. Watch for a *big, bulky, dark bird flying low and slow* over the reeds and rushes, especially near sunset or before dawn, when bitterns are most active. Try to discern where it lands.

2. Whether or not you've seen a bird, *sit in your vehicle* (it makes a great blind; even bitterns usually aren't suspicious of vehicles), with the engine off and the windows down. Listen for a bittern's distinctive, thumping call. When you hear one, either drive slowly towards it, if the road allows you to, or approach on foot, moving very slowly and stealthily, with frequent pauses.

3. Listen carefully for the sound of *two sharp clicks* at the beginning of the song, before the gulping, pumping sounds begin. That's the bittern snapping its beak, and it's a sound you'll hear only if you are close to the bird. Wait and watch, wait and watch.

4. Look for *reeds or swamp grass moving* when there is no breeze; a bittern may be parting the vegetation as it walks through.

5. Check the muddy edges of still water for *a brown lump* that doesn't match the vertical lines of the grasses and reeds. The bird may be standing perfectly still, only its active, darting eyes giving it away, or it may be stalking prey along the water's edge.

6. Fake a *series of loud coughs*. No, really. Sometimes a burst of noise can set off the denizens of a marsh, loosing an ech-

oing volley of whinnies from a secretive little sora or the clucking of a Virginia rail, with a bittern's *chunk*ing call soon to follow.

7. **Use binoculars,** even if the bittern sounds as if it's very nearby. Slowly scanning the suspected area with extra magnification will help you discern the body outline, the moving eyes, perhaps feet or legs, the slightest motion of stems, or other giveaways.

Once you successfully track down your first bittern, the next one will be easier. And so on, and so on.

Eventually, all those subtle signs will add up so quickly and subconsciously that you can home in on a vocalizing bittern in just a few minutes, without even thinking about it.

Lightening the Load

If you happen to take a bittern by surprise, duck and cover as soon as you get over the heart-stopping shock of a big bird flapping up from under your feet.

Like many other birds—even the finches or jays at your feeder—bitterns often "lighten the load" as they take off into the air.

When the heavy bird you've taken by surprise awkwardly tries to get airborne, it'll let out a loud croak—and suddenly discharge a huge splash of white excrement.

Seems like that's enough to help it settle into a slow, sturdy, determined flight across the marsh, its dark wings flapping low above the rushes.

Hunter Deluxe

> [11] *The Lord will be terrible unto them: for he will famish all the gods of the earth…*
>
> —Zephaniah 2:11

For the bittern, the usual state is well fed, not famished.

A bittern's sneaky habits are partly to keep the bird safe from predators. Foxes, coyotes, even larger hawks and eagles, are always on the lookout, and a big meaty fowl is prime pickings. Mmm, tastes like chicken…maybe?

But that stealthy way of moving, coupled with the now-you-see-me, now-you-don't camouflage, has another equally important purpose.

Bitterns are predators, and those furtive habits help these big birds fill their own bellies.

The Eclipse of the Sun-Gazer

In Louisiana, where bitterns are still common, although not as plentiful as they once were, Cajuns dubbed these birds *garde soleil*—sun-gazer—for their habit of standing with bill upstretched towards the sky. Cajuns also called them *grobek,* an onomatopoeic approximation of the pumping call. And they called them "food."

Before the American bittern was protected by federal law, the big, plump birds (weighing as much as a solid pound-and-a-half) were prized for eating, and many were shot in the swamps of Louisiana, the wetlands of New Jersey, and other places.

Today, bitterns aren't nearly as common as they used to be. The decline—which has been noted worldwide, in all species of bitterns—is partly blamed on hunting in years past (for both food and stuffed specimens), but that isn't the main reason, by far. The destruction of wetlands that has been going on for hundreds of years is the main reason for the decline of sun-gazers around the world.

Have you ever walked along the water's edge and heard the squeaks of frogs as they leap to safety?

Now, imagine you were walking in the glacially slow stalk of a bittern, your agile toes carefully high-stepping from one grip to another. A sudden stab with that rapier bill, and there goes the frog, right down the hatch.

The most bizarre bittern encounter I ever witnessed took place at a small, still pool in a backwater of the Columbia River in Washington state, at the Ridgefield National Wildlife Refuge.

The first thing that caught my eye was a happy family of muskrats, babies about the size of smallish guinea pigs splashing and diving in the dark water among some dabbling ducks.

I pulled my car over to sit and watch. That's when I finally noticed the bittern hunched on a low dead branch, watching the muskrats just as intently as I was. Its body was motionless, but its bright yellow eyes followed every movement.

Suddenly, a flurry of motion—the bittern had managed to snag a baby muskrat that had ventured too close. Mama Muskrat zoomed across the pond towards the bittern, teeth bared and chattering loudly, but to no avail.

Moving as quick as a snake, the bittern tossed its prey into the air, opened its bill wide to catch it on the way down, and swallowed it whole.

"Bitterns eat muskrats?" I wondered incredulously.

Yep, they sure do. And any other live prey they can catch. As with their cousins, the herons, bitterns have no interest in eating plants. These birds are hunters, and it's meat all the way, whether that meat is finned, scaled, or furred. Luckily for the baby animals of the marsh, insects make up a major part of the bittern's menu.

Only the Lonely

> [11] *The Lord will be terrible unto them: for he will famish all the gods of the earth; and men shall worship him, every one from his place, even all the isles of the heathen.*
>
> [12] *Ye Ethiopians also, ye shall be slain by my sword.*
>
> —Zephaniah 2:11-12

The third mention of the bittern in the Bible comes up in the book of Zephaniah, another prophet who foretells the wreaking of destruction upon the corrupt, especially upon Judah.

Reinforcing Isaiah's prophecy, Zephaniah details the gloomy scene:

> [14] *And flocks shall lie down in the midst of her, all the beasts of the nations: both the cormorant and the bittern shall lodge in the upper lintels of it; their voice shall sing in the windows;*

desolation shall be in the thresholds; for he shall uncover the
cedar work.

—Zephaniah 2:14

Now, here's a curiosity in the Scripture—a possible mistake?

Bitterns stalk the marshes with both feet firmly on the ground, occasionally grasping a stem or twig to secure better purchase in the slick footing of the marsh.

But lodging in the upper lintels? Hmm.

A lintel sits horizontally over the space of a doorway or window. Once God smote the cities, beams and lintels would be all that remained standing among the piles of rubble.

Cormorants? Sure. They often settle on the branches of trees.

A lintel wouldn't be a bad perch for a bittern, who could curl its long, jointed toes around the support to get a secure grip.

Except for one problem: American bitterns don't often perch at heights. Only a few instances have been recorded, ever.

Nope, if you want to see a bittern, you have to scour the marsh with your gaze at ground level.

On the other hand, night herons—who share a similar silhouette—often roost in trees. Maybe the prophet confused the two?

Or maybe, once the land was devoid of human inhabitants, bitterns might change their habits? With no watching eyes around anymore, maybe they would feel safe to sit on a perch where they're exposed to view.

Turns out, there's a much simpler explanation.

The bittern of the Bible would've been the Eurasian species, the great or yellow bittern. Unlike his North American cousin, this bird often perches in trees. And, we presume, would try out the new perches on lintels among the rubble of once-great Babylon.

Yet, like his American relative, the great bittern is also a recluse. It, too, lives in inaccessible marshes, preferring the company of its single self to a life lived with a companion.

Alone? Yes.

Lonely? Not if you're a bittern.

AMERICAN BITTERN
(*Botaurus lentiginosus*)

American range: Widely distributed over most of North America, but found only in marshes. Year-round in mild-winter regions; spring to fall, in others.

Natural diet: Fish, frogs, voles, mice, snakes, crayfish, eels, grasshoppers, and whatever other critters it can get into its dagger beak.

Feeder offerings: Not a feeder visitor.

Related species in the Bible area: Great bittern, sometimes called yellow bittern (*Botaurus stellaris*).

A note on translation: The Hebrew word *qā'āth* is translated "bittern" in the King James Version of the Bible; in the Douay-Rheims Version, the same word is inconsistently translated as "bittern," "cormorant," or "pelican."

Chapter 4

Raven

Feathered Genius

> [11] *His head is as the most fine gold, his locks are bushy, and black as a raven.*
>
> —Song of Solomon 5:11

Ravens are gleaming black, that's for sure. Their glossy plumage is usually the first thing we notice.

But it's the brains beneath those black feathers that call for even greater appreciation.

Ravens are smart.

Really smart.

Proportionately, their brains are the same size as those of whales and dolphins and of great apes—brainiacs, all. Not impressed? Okay, how about this: Ounce for ounce of body weight, raven brains are almost as big as our own.

All of their cousins in the Corvid family—crows, jays, magpies, nutcrackers, rooks, and jackdaws—are geniuses, too. They can solve problems, use tools, remember things to a degree that even we can't do, and figure out problems by using logic.

In other words, they *think*.

That's a rarity among birds. Indeed, among all animals. Most species depend on trial-and-error experimentation to figure out what's a good way to achieve a goal, and what's not. And that's been the demise of countless birds, animals, and other critters: Sometimes, the trial leads to a fatal error.

All birds are perfectly suited to their natural lives, of course. But only ravens and other corvids can use their thinking power to better their lot in life.

Saving for a Rainy Day

[24] *Consider the ravens: for they neither sow nor reap; which neither have storehouse nor barn; and God feedeth them: how much more are ye better than the fowls?*

—Luke 12:24

Uh, hang on a minute, please, Luke the Evangelist. We need to talk about those storehouses.

Ravens eat a lot of their food right on the spot. But they also put aside edibles for days when pickings may be slim.

That behavior is called *caching* (say CASH-ing, from the French *cacher*, "to press together, to hide"), and corvids are experts. They stash food in the top of dead snags, in old woodpecker holes, behind loose flaps of bark, in crevices in rocks, under dead leaves.

They're stocking the pantry. And then, in lean times, they come back to retrieve a meal from their larders.

Unlike the acorn woodpecker, which uses a single dead tree or utility pole to store thousands of nuts, corvids put their stuff in many different locations. And they remember where they put it. The American corvid known as Clark's nutcracker is the winner in this category—studies show that one of these obsessed, er, hard-working birds can cache 98,000 seeds in a single season and, even more incredibly, remember every one of its hiding places.

Corvids also are thieves. Or, to put it nicely, opportunists. By keeping an eye out for other birds carrying or caching food, they get many a fine meal second-hand.

If a raven suspects its cache has been discovered, it will move every morsel to another hiding place. The mere presence of a possible thief—and one knowing look—is enough to set off a raven into transferring the contents of one of its prized storehouses to a new secret location.

The Social Gaze

Ever notice how you "just know" when your spouse is wondering what happened to the remote control? Or how your dog seems to know when you're thinking about taking him for a walk or giving him a treat?

It's all in the eyes.

Some animals that live in social groups keep their eyes open, literally, tracking what scientists call the *social gaze.* They follow the direction of the eyes of other members of the group, in order to predict what will happen next.

Your spouse looking towards the coffee table, where the remote usually resides. The eyes of Fido's owner aimed at the hook where the dog leash hangs, or at the cookie jar of dog treats. Dead giveaway.

People, dogs, chimpanzees and other monkeys all use the social gaze. It's invaluable in these groups, where the behavior of one often affects the others.

Ravens do it, too. If a competitor is looking towards that treasured cache of food, for instance, the raven recognizes the target of that gaze and knows exactly what will happen next—thievery, and all that hard work for naught. Time to move the storehouse.

Caught Red-Handed

It's almost impossible to catch a raven in the act of caching food. With their clever brains and alert eyes, they make sure no one is watching when they hide that treasure.

Only once have I seen a raven hide its food, and even then I wasn't sure.

Husband Matt and I were feeding sliced bread to gulls on an Oregon beach when a raven came flying in and landed a little distance away.

Moving ever closer to the food, he kept his head up and strolled along as casual as could be.

"Not making a beeline for that bread, nope, not me!"

Uh huh. Mr. Innocent, all right.

When he'd approached close enough to the prize—without alarming any of the gulls that were also eating—he reached out and snatched the wadded lump of sliced bread, flapping his wings at the same time so he was airborne before the gulls had time to react. With plenty of food still on the sand, they didn't bother to give chase.

The raven flew about 50 yards to the high tide line on the beach, where driftwood, seaweed, and eelgrass were piled in a tangled, jumbled mass.

Turning his back on us—an action that looked deliberate, and may well have been—he probed into the pile here and there, always keeping his head out of our sight.

"What's he doing? Did he stash the bread?"

"Can't tell."

In a few minutes, the raven flew off into the nearby forest. With his head facing away from us, there was no way to see if he still held the bread in his bill when he left.

"Must've taken it back into the trees to eat."

"Maybe not."

We hiked over to the spot where the raven had spent some time doing whatever it was he'd been doing.

No bread visible, even when we peered intently into the jumbled debris.

Giving up, I settled on a log of driftwood to watch the ocean. But Matt was more determined. He kept searching.

"Aha!" He'd found the cache.

I hurried to his side and squinted at the flotsam and jetsam.

"I give up. Where?"

He pointed to a worn seagull feather atop the driftwood sticks. "See that feather? Must be his marker."

Sure enough.

A sand-speckled corner of bread was barely visible deep beneath the feather. Even when I knew exactly where it was, I still had difficulty relocating the cache after I briefly took my eyes off it.

Carefully, we lifted the grass and sticks on top. Yep. It was the entire lump, three or four slices of soft white bread shoved way down deep into the debris.

A quick photo, then we replaced the disguise.

No sign of the raven who'd hidden the food. But we were sure he was somewhere in the trees, keeping his sharp eyes on us.

With guile like that, it's no wonder Luke the Evangelist never realized that ravens do indeed have a storehouse.

Whether it's God or us who provide, ravens are smart enough to save some for a rainy day.

How Smart Is "Smart"?

Surrounded by miles and miles of bleak wilderness, Anchorage, Alaska, is an oasis. It beckons to ravens with abundant sources of easy food.

In the morning, about 2,000 of the birds fly into the city to visit their favorite feeding places—restaurant dumpsters, shopping malls, and other good scavenging sites.

Before dusk, they leave, streaming out of the city to nighttime roosts. Where are those roosts? No one could figure it out.

State biologist Rick Sinnott and his team decided to tag some of the birds with radio transmitters to find out exactly where they were spending the night. But first they had to catch them.

They started with a giant chicken-wire trap, 40 feet long and 5 feet high, baited with carcasses. The big black birds perched nearby and walked around it. No way were they going inside.

Next idea: Shoot a bird-catching net from a van at ravens who were gathered in parking lots or elsewhere. Success! Twenty-three birds were nabbed. But the net method didn't work for long. Birds that got away soon spread the word, and ravens began avoiding the van like the plague.

Next plan: Leghold traps, their jaws padded to be harmless but still keep a firm grip, buried under snow, with bright orange Cheetos® scattered atop for bait.

Ravens love Cheetos® as much as I do, and that first attempt caught 26 birds. Next time, though, ravens only perched or circled, looking longingly at the tasty snacks. But not a one came to dine.

The research into finding the big roost was pretty much a flop. The only roosts found were small ones—80 birds in a bridge support, and a few other smaller congregations outside the city. The mass of the 2,000 or so birds are still keeping their nightly accommodations a secret.

Smart. Very smart.

Super Scavengers

[41] Who provideth for the raven his food? when his young ones
cry unto God and wander for lack of meat.

—Job 38:41

Sometimes you just have to toot your own horn to open someone's eyes to all you do. And God did just that in Job 38, in which he asks question after question to which the only possible answer for Job is, "You do, God."

Ravens, just like all other living things on earth, do get their food. First stop for a filling meal: Often, along a roadway.

Meet the sanitation engineers of the bird world. Along with their relatives, the crows, magpies, and jays, and their fellow carrion-eaters, the vultures, ravens do yeoman work as garbage men.

Without them, the carcasses on our roadways and in the wild would build up fast. As would the trash from fast-food restaurants that uncaring folks toss out the window as they drive along.

And there's the rub.

Ravens quickly learned that the detritus of civilization holds plenty of promise for at least a quick bite, if not a full meal. They moved from their outposts in the wild world to take up residence in our cities and towns, where plenty of food is free for the picking.

Ravens are smart birds, the Mensa members of the bird world, along with their other relatives in the Corvid family.

Give them a problem, and they'll solve it.

They learned fast how to deal with getting at that good stuff.

Styrofoam™ takeout container? Flipping it open, no problem: Insert bill, and twist.

Fast-food bag? Grab with beak, and let 'er rip.

Didn't lock the lid down tight when you took the overstuffed trash can to the curb? A trash can lid is hardly a challenge for these birds, who persevere, levering a bit at a time, until that lid pops off.

Plastic trash bags that aren't in cans? Even easier: Just tear through that outer layer, and all the goodies are in full view.

That's why many folks, especially in cities and towns, consider ravens to be pests. They can turn a tidy bag of trash into a block-long trail of litter in minutes. Frustrating, for sure, but easily remedied: Just use cans and lock that lid down tight.

Counting on Ravens

"I set up a blind, hoping to photograph scavenging golden eagles," remembers Lou Bartmann, a nature lover in Colorado. Instead, he got a lesson in how good ravens are at math. But, here, let's let Lou tell the story:

"Got a cow's head from a rendering plant (the head fit nicely into the trunk of my trusty Ford Pinto), placed it about 40 feet from the blind, and put a shiny can lid on the blind where the camera lens would be.

"I waited a couple of days for the wildlife to get used to the changes. Big mistake. When I returned, the head was completely gone. Coyotes had hauled it away.

"Back to the rendering plant. This time they gave me a pig. I wrapped it with baling wire and drove in stakes to hold it down.

"After I was in the blind, two ravens came to a pine tree nearby. But they wouldn't come to the pig.

"A book I'd read said that the trick was to go to the blind with more than seven people—the author believed that ravens could add and subtract up to seven.

"If eight or more people go into the blind, then, when everyone except you leaves, the ravens will think it's safe.

"The next morning, a bunch of friends happened to come to visit, and I convinced them to go with me. There were 9 or 10 of us.

"It worked! After they left the blind, the ravens came to the pig within minutes. Though I never did get any good pictures."

Food for One, Food for All

¹⁵ Every raven after his kind;

—Leviticus 11:15

Ravens gladly devour live small animals, such as mice, whenever they're able to nab them. You may see a flock of ravens stabbing at meadow mice in an overgrown field, or following a combine in a wheat field to nab the rodents or small birds left in its tracks, or patrolling the edge of a pond, looking for frogs.

Grain will do, too, which is why ravens often settle in harvested cornfields or other farm areas where they can glean the leftovers.

But the main menu item for these super-intelligent birds is dead animals—carrion, as we call it.

And to chow down on that favored food, they have to depend on others to do the killing.

In today's world, cars play the main role. Those wheeled engines of death make it super easy for ravens.

Roadkill is abundant along just about every highway and byway, providing a smorgasbord of rabbits, squirrels, deer, even cattle in areas of the West where those hefty steaks-on-the-hoof range free without fences.

In prior times, though, the clever birds had to depend on predators to make the kill. And in remote areas, they still do.

Go for the Bold

Do ravens hang back, biding their time, when they spot predators at a kill?

It would be the safest choice, for sure. Even when busy at a fresh meal, predators are happy to stop eating the main course for a minute and grab a raven for a side dish.

Like magpies and crows, ravens often tag along with hunting wolves and coyotes. Bold as brass, but keeping a safe distance and ready to fly at a moment's notice, they sidle right up to the carcass, even when the toothy predators are still eating.

It sure isn't a leisurely dinner, but filling the belly is the objective. So this seemingly risky behavior pays off as the raven grabs its share of the feast.

If the ravens waited until those wolves or coyotes or bear (or in the Mideast, foxes, lions, or jackals) eventually move off for a post-prandial nap, there might be precious little left of the prey.

So ravens go bold.

Carefully, of course. And cleverly, as is their wont.

Testing the Limits

> [9] He giveth to the beast his food, and to the young ravens which cry.
>
> —Psalms 147:9

Psalms 147 hammers home the message we already heard in the book of Job, extolling all of the many things that God does. Including making sure ravens get fed.

If you're lucky enough to come across four-footed predators at a kill, you'll likely see both the "beasts" and the "young ravens" getting their food—and you'll notice how the canny ravens work the situation to their advantage.

One cold autumn day in Yellowstone National Park, I spotted movement far below in a meadow near the river. Finding a safe place to pull over, I focused my binoculars on the scene below. A pack of the famed Yellowstone gray wolves had taken down an elk and were busily feeding.

At first I watched only the wolves, because seeing them at all is such a rare treat. Then I noticed the ravens. There were at least half a dozen, with more arriving every minute.

Trial-and-Error? That's for Amateurs

Trial-and-error is the main method by which most birds figure things out. You've seen it yourself in your yard: Add a new kind of feeder, and the cardinals and chickadees will try it out until they have it nailed. That first approach may be comical as the birds flutter at the feeder—"Where's the perch?" "How do I get my beak on this food?"

Ravens, though, sit back and consider. By the time they're ready to give it a try, they know exactly how far to fly, where to get a secure foothold, and how to grab the goodies. Their attempt to get the food works the first time, because they've thought through the problem.

A couple of the birds were actively annoying the wolves—actually taking a quick nip at their hindquarters. As soon as the wolf whirled around, the raven was outta there, leaping backwards in great hops with half-opened wings.

It seemed to me the ravens were testing the limits, trying to determine exactly what distance would be enough to keep the wolves busy at their meal instead of trying to drive the bird away.

Live & Learn

Sure enough, Bernd Heinrich, who's been studying ravens his whole life, came to the same conclusion.

Older birds, he determined, have already learned just what that safe distance is, and they quickly settle in at the kill, maintaining a respectful boundary from the feeding predators.

It's younger ravens that are doing the risky nipping, noted Heinrich. They're learning just how far away they need to stay. And annoying the wolves is one sure way to figure that out.

"Ouch! Who's pulling my fur?!" One mistake, and that young raven could easily become the wolf's next meal.

Pulling a beast's hair serves another purpose—it lets other ravens swiftly grab a bite while the predator is distracted.

Creating a Distraction

I've seen equally smart raven behavior up here at our home in the Rockies, where we put out food for our meat-eating birds—ravens, magpies, and jays—in a fenced garden enclosure in winter, when the bears are sleeping.

One day, I forgot to close the gate when I left the day's offering of roast turkey remains and most of a pan of leftover lasagna.

The ravens, magpies, and jays quickly settled at the food.

Soon after, a big coyote who happened to be passing through caught the scent. Looking around warily, he entered the fenced area to feed.

Far and Wide

Ravens are strong fliers that can and do cover a lot of ground. Much of their flight is simply soaring, without flapping, as they let the air currents do the work.

The home territory varies hugely in size, depending on the amount of food the birds can find. Abundant food, and the claimed area may be only 10 square miles or less. Hard to find food, and the birds require a much larger territory.

In areas where ravens depend on natural food, not human leftovers, the big birds spend a large part of their time scouting for edibles from the sky. Soaring 100 miles in a day is child's play for ravens, who can easily coast on the wind without flapping. Some ravens go to much greater lengths: Scientists have tracked banded birds regularly traveling more than 700 miles back and forth.

The magpies and jays who'd been picking at the meat quickly retreated to the fence to survey the situation.

But the ravens were having none of that—this was their breakfast, and the coyote was eating it. Although they flew up when the coyote moved in, they quickly got the better of him.

One raven landed in full view of the coyote, strutting and scolding to distract the animal from the food. The other raven swooped in low from behind, quickly walked to the lasagna, and snatched as big a hunk as it could carry—about twice the size of a typically generous Italian restaurant portion, a solid chunk that must've weighed close to a pound.

By this time, the coyote realized something was up. Whipping around, he lunged at the sneaky raven by the lasagna.

Too late. Both ravens were already flapping away, towards a nearby tree. There they settled side by side, anchoring the lasagna with a steadying foot, while they took turns sharing the spoils.

Unsavory Snacks

> [17] *The eye that mocketh at his father, and despiseth to obey his mother, the ravens of the valley shall pick it out, and the young eagles shall eat it.*
>
> —Proverbs 30:17

Big sinister birds that show little fear of humans? And avidly eat flesh? Now, there's the stuff of nightmares.

Better be good, kids.

Ravens are omnivores, which means they eat just about anything. No salads, thanks, but plenty of meat, dead or alive, plus grains and fish and insects, with a side helping of berries or fruit.

These are big birds—2 feet from stem to stern, with a wingspan from 3½ to 5 feet, and tipping the scales at nearly 3 pounds (a hummingbird, by contrast, weighs about as much as a penny).

Sinister? You Bet!

A direct threat is easier to deal with, psychologically, than a creature that sits and waits, watching, watching, watching.

If an aggressive dog, a bear, or even a mountain lion targets us, we can wave our arms, throw a rock, holler as loud as we can, and maybe chase it away.

Adrenaline kicks in when our life is directly threatened, and we do what we must. Which, by the way, should not be "Run!" That would excite the prey-chasing instinct of a four-legged threat, and we'd be dead meat before we knew it.

Ravens, on the other hand, aren't about to beat their wings at us in a frenzy, nor peck us to death. We're way bigger than they are.

But let's imagine we're staggering across a desolate desert, hoping to reach the oasis. Not such a far-fetched scenario in Bible days, or even today—hikers still get lost in dire circumstances.

Ravens spot us from the sky. They gather on nearby rocks or settle in trees, gauging our weakness. Aha! Now that two-legged creature is crawling! Now it's stopped! Time to investigate....

That wait-and-watch behavior can be pretty unsettling, if you're the focus. Even when the big black birds are only gathered near the bird feeder or the trash can, they look ominous. Maybe because our minds know what they're capable of.

By patrolling from the air, ravens have an advantage over the four-legged diners, which have to depend on sense of smell or happenstance.

Should a raven happen to be first on the scene, it goes for the easiest-access food first. Its bill isn't strong enough to rip through animal hide. And besides, ravens are just like the rest of us—they take the easy route.

The Most Tender Morsel

If the body is intact, any bit of soft tissue will serve as an entry point.

What's the softest tissue of all? Eyeballs. Which give direct access into the oh-so-tasty brain.

Yes, this all sounds perfectly awful, and not something we even want to think about.

But the Bible warning of Proverbs 30:17 (*"...the ravens of the valley shall pluck it out..."*) rings absolutely true.

Picking out the eyes is perfectly natural behavior for ravens. Sometimes, the animal behind those eyeballs isn't even dead yet— attacks on lambs have been recorded.

Be nice to your mother and father, and you won't have to worry about those Proverbial eyeball-plucking ravens.

After the Flood

> [17] And, behold, I, even I, do bring a flood of waters upon the earth, to destroy all flesh, wherein is the breath of life, from under heaven; and every thing that is in the earth shall die.
>
> [18] But with thee will I establish my covenant; and thou shalt come into the ark, thou, and thy sons, and thy wife, and thy sons' wives with thee.
>
> [19] And of every living thing of all flesh, two of every sort shalt thou bring into the ark, to keep them alive with thee; they shall be male and female.
>
> —Genesis 6:17-19

Rain, rain, go away... and after 40 days and 40 nights, it finally did. Yet Noah's Ark, a refuge for people and animals during the Great Flood, was still surrounded by water as far as the eye could see.

Patiently, the precious cargo waited. And waited.

Finally, Noah sent out a bird, to see if maybe, by now, there might be a bit of land above the water.

A dove?

Nope. Not the first time.

> *6 And it came to pass at the end of forty days, that Noah opened the window of the ark which he had made:*
>
> *7 And he sent forth a raven, which went forth to and fro, until the waters were dried up from off the earth.*
>
> —Genesis 8:6-7

The raven never returned to the Ark.

Why? Eating habits. Ravens eat just about anything, whether it's plant, animal, or insect. Scavenging is their stock in trade. The raven was no doubt happily flexing its wings and enjoying a banquet as the waters receded.

Okay, no report from the raven. Noah tried again, this time with a dove. No luck, the first time:

> *9 But the dove found no rest for the sole of her foot, and she returned unto him into the ark, for the waters were on the face of the whole earth: then he put forth his hand, and took her, and pulled her in unto him into the ark.*
>
> —Genesis 8:9

Patience. Third try's the charm:

> *10 And he stayed yet other seven days; and again he sent forth the dove out of the ark;*
>
> *11 And the dove came in to him in the evening; and, lo, in her mouth was an olive leaf pluckt off: so Noah knew that the waters were abated from off the earth.*
>
> — Genesis 8:10-11

Why did the dove return, even though the floodwaters were disappearing?

Doves eat only seeds (and fruit, for some species). And since the world had just been under water, the bird had to return to the Ark, its sole source of food, until plants again had a chance to grow and set seed or bear fruit. As for that olive leaf, you can read about Noah's dove and its habits in Chapter 11 of this book.

Taking on Civilization

[11] But the cormorant and the bittern shall possess it; the owl also and the raven shall dwell in it: and he shall stretch out upon it the line of confusion, and the stones of emptiness.

—Isaiah 34:11

Isaiah was talking about the devastation that God was planning to wreak upon the sinful kingdom of Judah.

The raven was a fitting symbol of desolate isolation in those times, when its dark shadow swept across deserts and rocky cliffs but never ventured near civilization.

But ravens have moved on. Nowadays, they're right at home among the bustling millions of Los Angeles, Washington, D.C., Portland, Oregon, the suburbs of cities, and other human haunts.

Not all of them have made the leap, though.

Ravens are still common in the wildest of wild places—the deepest, darkest forests and highest mountaintops of the Appalachians (where they were reintroduced), Rockies, Cascades, and Sierras; the merciless deserts of the American Southwest; the icy cold Far North. You'll still hear their croaking calls, far from any human habitation, as they soar overhead, wheeling on rising air currents.

But the lure of food has also drawn them to towns and cities.

"Would you like fries with that?"

Oh, you can't eat it all? Great! Leftovers for the ravens.

Speaking of Food

> [12] *But these are they of which ye shall not eat: the eagle, and the ossifrage, and the ospray,*
>
> [13] *And the glede, and the kite, and the vulture after his kind;*
>
> [14] *And every raven after his kind;*
>
> [15] *And the owl, and the night hawk, and the cuckow, and the hawk after his kind;*
>
> [16] *The little owl, and the great owl, and the swan,*
>
> [17] *And the pelican, and the gier eagle, and the cormorant,*
>
> [18] *And the stork, and the heron after her kind, and the lapwing, and the bat.*

—Deuteronomy 14:12-18

And just in case you didn't get the message, the same stern warning is repeated almost word for word in Leviticus 11:13-19.

Notice a theme here?

All of these birds eat other animals, alive or dead.

Carrion eaters are not approved. Birds of prey are a no-no, too. Major fish-eaters, sorry, not for supper.

Bats? Well, they're not "fowls," that's for sure, but they do have wings, and some species drink blood.

This list was written thousands of years ago, as were the similar prescriptions in the Jewish Talmud and Muslim Q'uran, yet even today it still seems sensible to us.

We don't dine on rotisseried owls or breast of pelican, and the thought of eating a raven or heron is enough to turn our stomachs.

Interestingly, while the Bible decrees clean and unclean animals by virtue of their physical characteristics—cloven hoofs, chewing cuds—it lists the birds by name.

Could be that's because there are way more kinds of birds than there are animals.

Eat This, Not That

Food laws are common in religions, and the Bible is no exception. Many of the rules seem like simple common sense today, when we consider what science now knows about the diseases or parasites the "unclean" animals may be carrying.

Yes, bacon is mighty tasty, and baby back ribs are hard to resist.

But those pigs that begat our bacon might have been infected with trichinosis, a nasty parasite that eagerly takes up residence in our own intestines.

Trichinosis, salmonella, and other diseases that can pass into people are also carried by wild game, including many of the animals that fall into the Bible's "do not eat" list.

Many Bible scholars have theorized that the dietary restrictions delineated in Deuteronomy and Leviticus appear to have their root in the eating habits or the diseases and parasites that may be possibly transmitted by the animals.

The restrictions would have helped protect people from diseases that these critters might be carrying.

The Middle East is a vast flyway. Millions and millions of birds—maybe a billion or more—from Europe, Asia, and Africa pour through in spring and in fall.

More than 200 species of birds nest in Israel alone, and another 334 or so species pass through on their way to other homes.

Palestine, Jordan, Syria, Egypt, and other modern countries that made up the lands of the Bible are just as rich in birdlife.

With numbers like that, plus the difficulty of differentiating 500 species by food habits or physical characteristics, it's a lot easier to list the handful of "thou shalt not" birds than it would've been to make generalizations.

Memorize the cheat sheet in Leviticus or Deuteronomy, and

you'll be walking on the right side of God's law. And you'll still have hundreds of kinds of birds around that you can gulp right down the hatch.

So go right ahead, lick your chops at the sight of a lake teeming with ducks and geese, a flock of doves, a nice fat pheasant (yes, they're native birds in the Middle East), or a covey of plump scuttling quail.

They, along with many, many other birds, aren't included on the "do not eat" list.

Black as Night

[11] His head is as the most fine gold, his locks are bushy, and black as a raven.

—Song of Solomon 5:11

The loving couple in Song of Solomon used the raven's color as a compliment.

But when you combine the awareness of a raven with its large size and its all-black feathers, you've got a bird that seems so sinister, it's featured in folklore as a sign of evil or impending doom.

It's all in the eye of the beholder.

Ravens are just doing natural raven things. No malice intended, even when one of the big birds seems to be staring intently at your eyes as if they're *hors d'oeuvres.*

As for that pitch-black color, that, too, is in our own beholding eyes. Our human eyes can only see colors that fall in what's called the *visible spectrum.* We can't see ultraviolet colors, unless we use a special light to make them visible.

Not so with ravens.

Like other birds, they're able to see the ultraviolet light spectrum, as well as the spectrum visible to our more restricted vision.

The black birds may all look alike to us. But ravens, with their ultraviolet vision, can see the difference.

Those black feathers have markings that are invisible to our eyes. Ultraviolet markings, which differ between male and female birds. Ravens see them clearly.

But even our eyes can detect the iridescence of a raven's plumage. In the right light, those shining black feathers—especially on wings and tail—give off glints of green, deep blue, or purple.

And that's where a sharp-eyed human bird-lover can distinguish the girls from the boys: Adult females (which are also usually a bit smaller than males) show less purple on their body feathers than males, with wider dull black centers in the feathers.

On the breast or back feathers, that narrow purple edge, combined with the faded black of the rest of the feather, can give a female raven an almost scaly look. Even with our lack of ultraviolet sight, we can still tell the girls from the boys. Maybe.

Cooperation Counts

[3] *Get thee hence, and turn thee eastward, and hide thyself by the brook Cherith, that is before Jordan.*

—1 Kings 17:3

God was on the rampage again, because of the bad behavior of King Ahab and his wife, Jezebel.

This time it was a drought, a bad drought, a drought that would dry up the land and kill the wicked people.

No rain, not even any dew.

No doubt a slow, lingering, horrible death—but one that would wipe the kingdom clean and make it ready for a fresh start.

And Elijah the Prophet was right in the way. He lived in the neighborhood that was slated for demolition.

Fear not, Elijah: God had a plan to save his life. A plan that required cooperation from the ravens.

⁴ *And it shall be, that thou shalt drink of the brook; and I have commanded the ravens to feed thee there.*

—1 Kings 17:4

The Corvid family is well known for stealing from each other—but when cooperation is called for, they jump in right away to help each other out.

Usually, it's only other members of the same family that get the helping hand. And sometimes only the same species.

Let a predator appear on the scene, and corvids of all kinds—crows, ravens, jays, magpies, all of the relatives—come squawking.

If it's a hawk in the air, they'll dive at the dangerous bird, pecking and pulling out feathers.

If the predator is perched, perhaps an owl roosting in daytime, it's time for a mass dive-bombing by a gang of corvid pals until the predator leaves the branch and tries to flee.

Same thing with a good banquet, say, a moose or a deer. Too much for one bird to eat, so the first one to spot it loudly calls in the troops to share the bounty.

Corvids even cooperate when it comes to family life.

All of these intelligent birds mate for life, which in the case of ravens, may be a decade or more.

Raven offspring don't breed until they're two to three years old, and the birds from last year's nest sometimes stick around to act as nannies to the new batch.

When the nest of hungry nestlings is running the parents ragged with their "Feed me! NOW!" demands, the older progeny have been known to step in to lend their efforts.

Scientists call this *cooperative breeding,* and while it's been more commonly observed in jays and other smaller corvids, ravens have also been known to engage in such helpfulness.

They're ultra-secretive around the nest, though. If a human is in the area, the parents may flat-out refuse to approach.

And don't think they won't see you—ravens are so intelligent and so hyper-aware that very little escapes their notice. So collecting data on cooperative breeding in raven families—not to mention other aspects of raven life—can be quite a challenge.

Slackers, Get in Gear!

Researchers have noticed that some members of a group of corvids are often "lazier" than others, or at least that's how it looks at first glance. Turns out, they're the backup. So maybe they're just saving their energy.

In a study of European carrion crows, the non-breeding "helpers" fell into two categories: Those with a strong work ethic, and those who leaned more to the slacker side.

Although the slackers hung out with the community of carrion crows, they avoided ever visiting the needy nest.

Observations eventually showed that the slacker group was actually a backup bunch, for insurance. When they were needed, after a hard-working member was lost, they kicked into gear, working their tails off to feed the nestlings.

Goes to show there's hope for all of us.

Helping Hand or Happenstance?

> [5] *So he went and did according unto the word of the Lord: for he went and dwelt by the brook Cherith, that is before Jordan.*
>
> —1 Kings 17:5

Back to Elijah's story, and the terrible drought that God brought upon the land.

Water would have been a precious commodity in that parched landscape described in the first book of Kings.

So it's reasonable to think that the ravens would've spent time hanging out at Elijah's hideout at the brook—the only oasis around.

It doesn't take long for clever ravens to realize someone is not a threat. Although they would probably still have been wary, they may have accepted Elijah as part of the family, or, at least, not an enemy. Food was super abundant, thanks to the major die-off in the drought, so there would've been plenty to share.

> [6] *And the ravens brought him bread and flesh in the morning,*
> *and bread and flesh in the evening; and he drank of the brook.*

—1 Kings 17:6

Would ravens bring food to an individual that wasn't of their own species? Anecdotal accounts exist of tame ravens and crows feeding dogs or other pets, and my own pet crow would often bring me gifts of dead mice.

Did the ravens deliberately bring food to Elijah? It's possible.

Or did they bring their finds to the brook to dip in the water or eat at leisure, and Elijah survived by sharing their leftovers?

Another plausible explanation based on natural behavior.

Slam Dunk

Like a kid eating cookies and milk, ravens and crows often dip their food in water before they gulp it down. Why? Because wet food is easier to swallow.

Ranchers in the American West sometimes complain about ravens fouling the water troughs of livestock—when the big birds dunk their food, pieces fall off and decay in the water, making it unpalatable to the cattle or horses.

You can see the same behavior with ravens at any body of water—seacoast, river, lake, even a pond or creek.

But, as in other parts of their private lives, ravens usually only engage when they believe they're unobserved. Keep your head turned and watch out of the corner of your eye, for a better chance at seeing a raven do a dunk.

Play Is the Proof

>[20] *Curse not the king, no not in thy thought; and curse*
> *not the rich in thy bedchamber: for a bird of the air shall*
> *carry the voice, and that which hath wings shall*
> *tell the matter.*

—Ecclesiastes 10:20

"Psst! You hear about…?"

"You're kidding! Wow, really? How'd you find out?"

"Oh, a little bird told me."

This verse in Ecclesiastes is a great reminder to keep our lips sealed. Whatever we say, even in privacy, can travel far and fast.

But those secrets might have a hard time being spread, if we left it up to the ravens to carry the message. Because, when it comes to these big birds—well, their way of life isn't "all work and no play."

Ravens and other corvids are thinkers, scientists agree.

- They demonstrate being able to consider the future.
- They solve problems through logic.
- They fashion tools when they can't access the food.
- And they work together, combining forces when they have a common goal. Or a common enemy.

But the most endearing proof of their high intelligence?

They play.

Aerial Acrobatics

When we're talking about birds with a silly streak, ravens are right at the top of the list.

Whenever the mood strikes, and the wind is right, they put on an air show, doing loop-de-loops and somersaults, playing tag, diving and pulling up, and even flying upside down.

One particularly talented or maybe just goofy bird was seen flying upside down for more than half a mile. And ravens often fly upside down—for shorter stretches—as part of their aerial court-ship maneuvers.

Often, a raven who gets the urge to play will snap off a stick and invite his colleagues to an aerial game of pitch-and-catch.

Or drop-and-grab, to be more exact: The stick-holder suddenly releases the toy, then swoops it up before another raven can make the grab. The game may be played by a single bird, or by a group.

If you're lucky enough to have ravens visiting your yard—some might not call this "good" luck—you may even see them teasing your pets. A favorite game seems to be tugging a bit of hair while the dog is sleeping. You can almost hear the bird saying, "Wasn't me!" as it flies off, laughing.

COMMON RAVEN
(*Corvus corax*)

American range: Across most of North America.

Natural diet: In large part, carrion; also grains, insects, berries and fruit, small animals, and nestling birds. Human food, scavenged from trash, is always a favorite, if ravens are in the area.

At the feeder: If you have ravens in your neighborhood, try meat scraps, leftovers, bread and pastries, dried corn, and dry dogfood. We've learned they love lasagna and other cooked pasta, too.

American species: Common raven; Chihuahuan raven.

Raven species in the Bible area: Three species of ravens roam the Middle East: the common raven, same as our species, plus the brown-necked raven (*Corvus ruficolis*) and the fan-tailed raven (*Corvus rhipidurus*).

A note on translation: The Hebrew word '*orebh* means "black one," and may apply to magpies, crows, or jays, as well as to ravens. All are corvids, which share similar habits of behavior.

Chapter 5

Birds of Prey

Eyes in the Sky

> [11] *And when the fowls came down upon the carcases, Abram drove them away.*
>
> —Genesis 15:11

No matter which version of the Bible you read, you'll see that the Scriptures are mighty short on specifics on birds of prey.

Except for many references to eagles (yep, everyone recognizes an eagle, or thinks they do), plus the occasional shout-out to vultures (or falcons, depending on translation), they're all lumped together as "birds" or "fowls" or "birds of prey."

Why the mishmash?

No need to make much differentiation, since most species share similar habits. They're all meat eaters. And great fliers.

The main point of the Scriptures in which they're mentioned is usually to evoke sharp vision, superior strength, or to remind readers about their cleanup duties on dead animals...including the bodies of people who don't heed those Biblical warnings.

So what if a bird-lover like me pulls her hair out wanting to know *which* bird of prey we're talking about? Especially since the

Bible lands are so rich with scores of fascinating species?

"*Machs nichts*," as my father used to say. That's Pennsylvania Dutch for "Doesn't matter." We get the point of the verses, even without specific names.

As for those "carcases," they were the remains of the animals that Abraham (Abram) sacrificed when he made his covenant with God—a heifer, she-goat, ram, turtledove, and pigeon. A real feast for flesh-eating birds, and the "fowls" were ready and waiting.

Rapacious Raptors

When we think of "birds of prey," we think of tearing beaks, fierce talons, far-seeing eyes—birds that hunt living critters from above.

Falcons, hawks, eagles are all birds of prey that hunt in the daytime, or *raptors*. And they're the ones we think of first.

Ospreys go into this category, too, though they stick to fish.

Kites look and fly something like way overgrown swallows, with a dancing, buoyant flight. But they're also birds of prey. Even if, like our Everglades kite, all they eat is snails.

Vultures? Yep, they're birds of prey, or raptors, too, despite a diet that mostly depends on dead things.

Sorting Them Out

> [15] *[T]here shall the vultures also be gathered, every one with her mate.*
> —Isaiah 34:15

You'd think hawks, eagles, and vultures would be easy to sort out.

These are big birds, and they hang out right in the open, often in the air or perched in plain view.

Go ahead, try it. What's that big dark body perched atop the tree—a red-tailed hawk? A red-shouldered? A rough-legged?

Ha. Lots of luck. Usually, it takes a look with binoculars and a field guide close at hand—one that includes pictures of the many possible plumage variations within a single species—to determine the fine points that distinguish one bird of prey from another.

Oh! But look at that great big one soaring over there. Surely that must be an eagle!

Maybe. Or maybe not.

Many a time, I've called a vulture or a red-tailed hawk an eagle. Never vice versa, because a real eagle is simply unmistakable. Well, except for the time I mistook a pair of eagles for vultures. From a distance, with no way to judge size, other than "big," a vulture or hawk can look enough like an eagle to be pegged wrong.

When Is an Eagle Not an Eagle?

> [28] *For wheresoever the carcase is, there will the eagles be gathered together.*
>
> —Matthew 24:28

Now we get to the real problem with birds of prey in the Bible. In that part of the world, vultures look even more like eagles than our North American guys do.

The "Old World" vultures of the Middle East are closely related to eagles. Some species easily outclass various eagles in terms of size. Those vultures—including the lammergeyer, or bearded vulture, which some Bible translations refer to by name, maybe because it invokes such a scarily big bird—are downright huge, with wings up to 9½ feet across.

And, unlike our common and abundant turkey vulture, Old World vultures fly with their wings held straight out, not tilted up in a V. Same as eagles. So getting the two confused is even more understandable.

More than 50 different kinds of birds of prey are found in Palestine, Egypt, Israel, and other Bible lands. And yet, the Bible has only seven Hebrew words for these fascinating birds:

Hebrew transliteration	English translation
'ā·yiṭ	A collective term, meaning "birds of prey," although the King James Bible usually translates it as "fowls."
dã'ah or *dáyyah*	Most translations agree this word indicates a kite.
néshér	Generally, "eagle." Although large species of Old World vultures are often included under the blanket term.
'ay·yāh	Vulture. Or perhaps "buzzard," which in the Mideast means a bulky *Buteo* hawk, not a true Old World vulture.
rã'ah	A particular Old World vulture, probably the griffon.
ḏay·yō·wṯ	"Buzzards." That is, buteo hawks, not vultures.
neç	All falcons and smaller hawks are grouped under this one word.

Finding the Right Word

> [7] There is a path which no fowl knoweth, and which the
>   vulture's eye hath not seen.
>
>   —Job 28:7

Why did the Bible use interchangeable language for vultures and birds of prey like eagles? Because, in the Old World, these big birds belong to the same family. They look a lot alike in the air.

So the translators of the various versions took matters into their own hands. No doubt they looked closely at the context of each verse that mentioned these birds, in order to narrow it down.

But the translators may have been thinking of the birds in their own country (for the King James Version, that'd be England), rather than those of the Bible lands. Or they may have been unfamiliar with the habits of birds.

So they disagreed widely, which makes for some interesting reading of the same verses.

Consider Job 28, a chapter that describes a hidden mine, full of treasures, with a path that leads to it.

How to get there?

Uh, sorry, says God, it's a secret, not even known to the birds.

The 16—yes, 16—words of Job 28:7 vary so much from one translation of the Bible to another that it drove me to try to learn Hebrew. At least, enough Hebrew to look at the original and try to figure out how we got so many different versions.

In the King James version, which we've used throughout this book, the verse is: *There is a path which no fowl knoweth, and which the vulture's eye hath not seen.*

In the American Standard version, the same verse contradicts King James' translation: *That path no bird of prey knoweth, Neither hath the falcon's eye seen it.*

Fowl or bird of prey? Vulture or falcon?

Maybe a third version will help us decide. How about the Douay-Rheims? *The bird hath not known the path, neither hath the eye of the vulture beheld it.*

New International? *No bird of prey knows that hidden path, no falcon's eye has seen it.*

Bible in Basic English? *No bird has knowledge of it, and the hawk's eye has never seen it.*

Good News Translation? *No hawk sees the roads to the mines, And no vulture ever flies over them.*

Maybe the Revised Standard Version will finally sort this out.

That path no bird of prey knows, and the falcon's eye has not seen it.

Great! "Bird of prey" definitely carries the day for Bird #1 in the verse.

As for Bird #2, that's 3 votes for vulture, 3 for falcon, and 1 for hawk.

One more to tip the scales? Here's the Darby Translation: *It is a path no bird of prey knoweth, and the vulture's eye hath not seen it.*

Okay! Vultures win.

Well, unless those "birds of prey" we thought were settled suddenly become vultures, and "vultures" turn into hawks, as in the Message Bible, which was completed in 2002: *Vultures are blind to its riches, hawks never lay eyes on it.*

"Good Lord," one might cry after all this, "doesn't anyone know how to translate the original words?"

Short answer: No.

Lost in Translation

Remember the old kids' game, in which you'd whisper into someone's ear, they'd whisper the same thing into the ear of the next person, and so on? We called it "Whisper Down the Alley"; others call it "Telephone."

By the time the last person in the line spoke the words out loud, the message was nowhere near what you'd started with.

Bible translations can be a lot like that.

Some translations, including the King James, started from the original language.

But even those words aren't always clear, especially when it comes to birds. There's lots of room for disagreement over what one word or another should be.

Add in the fact that many Bible versions were written from already existing translations—which may have been in Hebrew, in Greek, in Aramaic, in Latin, in Old English, in modern English, in German, and I'm sure I've missed some.

No wonder the names of birds of prey are a tangled mess.

Like many another translator wannabe, I went back to the original to see if I could figure it out.

One Step from the Original

After struggling to decipher the subtleties of the Hebrew language, I gave up and moved on to the transliteration of those Hebrew words—their spelling in the English alphabet.

And there's the very first problem: Unless we can read Hebrew, we have to depend on a translation right from the get-go.

The Hebrew language does not use the characters of our English alphabet. So Hebrew words are "transliterated" into the letters we're familiar with.

The transliterated Hebrew word for the first bird in that line from Job 28:2 is *'ā·yiṭ*. The second bird, *'ay·yāh*.

At least the translators of the various versions were consistent (well, mostly). Wherever *'ā·yiṭ* shows up in the King James Version, it becomes "fowl." Wherever *'ay·yāh* perches on the page, it becomes "vulture."

Is there a falcon in the King James Version? Why, no. No, there is not.

No, there is not, despite the dozen species of falcons that range throughout the Bible lands.

Nope, no falcons here.

Other versions of the Bible may translate *'ay·yāh* as "falcon," but the King James staff was having none of that. Nope. In the King James Version, those things were vultures. That's their story, and they're sticking with it.

Except that I'm a stickler, when it comes to words. And vulture/hawk/falcon *does* make a difference, at least to my mind. I want to be able to picture the right birds—and what they're doing—whether I'm reading the Bible, or any other book.

Leftovers Don't Last Long

Birds of prey are super-abundant in the lands of the Bible.

To really grasp how many birds of prey these two countries have, keep in mind that the Israel of today is only 263 miles long, and 9 to 71 miles wide—less than 8,000 square miles in area.

Israel would fit with room to spare in our small state of Massachusetts. As for Texas, well, that big state could hold 33 Israels.

Today's Palestine is even smaller: about 5,600 square miles.

Take a look at this amazing list of birds of prey (compiled from Avibase; www.avibase.bsc-eoc.org), and think about how very small those countries are, compared to the whole of the United States.

Yep, that's a lot of flesh-eaters.

Comparison of Birds of Prey in Israel, Palestine, and the U.S.

Israel	Palestine	United States
2 honey-buzzards	2 honey-buzzards	0
3 kites	2 kites	5, most confined to small ranges
5 vultures	5 vultures	3 (turkey, black, California condor)
11 eagles	9 eagles	2 (bald; and golden, which we share with Israel and Palestine)
5 accipiters	3 accipiters	3 (sharp-shinned and Cooper's hawks, northern goshawk)
3 buteos (called "buzzards" in Israel)	3 buteos (called "buzzards" in Palestine)	12 (the familiar red-tailed hawk and others)
4 harriers	4 harriers	1 harrier
12 falcons	11 falcons	7 (we share the peregrine falcon with Israel and Palestine)
a few miscellaneous species, including the osprey	a few miscellaneous species, including the osprey	1 (the osprey)
TOTAL 57+	TOTAL 53+	TOTAL 33

Why, You Old Buzzard!

> [15] *[T]here shall the vultures also be gathered, every one with her mate.*
> —Isaiah 34:15

Or, as other translations of the Bible say, "buzzards," "hawks," or "kites" will be gathered there.

Isn't a buzzard a vulture?

Only in North America.

Call a bird of prey a "buzzard" in the Mideast or Europe, and you're talking about a *Buteo* hawk—the same genus as our robust red-tailed and red-shouldered and rough-legged hawks. Definitely not a vulture of any sort, as we know the word.

In the U.S., the word "buzzard" is synonymous with vulture. It's still in common usage in many parts of the country.

Not so in the Bible lands.

Which bird did the Bible actually mean in this quote? Any hawk, vulture, or kite will do, since the purpose was to point out a nesting place in the desolation after the destruction of Babylon.

But although all of these birds nest in uninhabited places, the King James Version's choice of "vultures" makes it sound even more ominous.

Dead or Alive

> [11] *And when the fowls came down upon the carcases, Abram drove them away.*
>
> —Genesis 15:11

Interestingly, in light of our look at the language of vultures, eagles, fowls, and falcons, no translators of any Bible version seem to have used the word "vultures" in this passage.

What do you know! This time there could be a good reason.

Hawks of various species, particularly the large buteos (of which our common red-tailed hawk is one) are just as happy to feast upon carrion as to make their own kills.

So are the most regal of eagles.

With one important difference: Vultures will eagerly eat just about anything, no matter how long it's been laying around. Eagles and hawks prefer their dead meat on the fresh side.

Years ago, I lived near a big turkey farm. Periodically, the owners would bring out the old manure spreader wagon and scatter the remains of their butchered birds over the farm fields as fertilizer. The spread covered acres at a time.

And the rain of white feathers from the wagon was the dinner bell, the signal for all of the vultures in the area to descend.

But not only vultures.

Strewn with white turkey feathers, the fields were soon peppered with the big dark forms of red-tailed hawks, rough-legged hawks, and even some bald eagles and golden eagles.

I'd seen plenty of vultures working on roadkill and other carcasses.

But it was a brand-new experience to watch the big hawks and eagles lurching about on the uneven ground, fighting over the tempting buffet of feathered bits.

We usually think of these superb hunters as proud, haughty, elegant—the royalty, if you will, of the bird world. Dealing death to their prey, as they plummet from the sky. And the Bible concurs, often using the eagle as a symbol of God himself.

Up until then, I'd only seen eagles perched or flying.

Time to adjust my own perspective.

They weren't "superior" to other birds. They weren't royal or elegant or any other special adjective I wanted to dub them with.

Those eagles and hawks were just birds, doing normal bird things. Which is, take advantage of easy food wherever they find it.

Or, as Luke quoted God (Luke 17:37), *"Wheresoever the body is, thither will the eagles be gathered together."*

How the Eagle-Eyed See

> [3] *And say, Thus saith the Lord God; A great eagle with great
> wings, longwinged, full of feathers, which had divers colours,
> came unto Lebanon, and took the highest branch of the cedar:*
>
> —Ezekiel 17:3

A high vantage point is where you'll find birds of prey. Kings of all
they survey, they sit patiently, their keen eyes ready to catch the
slightest movement.

That keenness of eye begins with the eyes themselves: They're
big. Not as large as those of owls, which have to gather what little
light there is at night. But bigger than the eyes of most other daytime birds.

All the better for seeing.

And that's only the start.

Those big eyes have lots and lots of receptors in the retina—
receptors that "read" the images transmitted by light. A diminutive
little kestrel has about twice as many receptors as we do in each
eye. A buteo hawk, five times more than we do.

The more receptors, the sharper the vision.

If that kestrel were perched atop a 60-foot tree, it could spot a fruitfly on the ground.

And then things get even better.

In the middle of the retina is a structure called the fovea, which is super-jam-packed with receptors.

Guess what? Birds of prey have not just one fovea in each eye, as we do. They have two. One for forward view, one for side view. Extra sharp vision, no matter which way the bird is looking.

But wait! There's more!

It's not only the number of receptors that give birds of prey their superior vision, it's how those eyes work together—which is, just like a pair of binoculars.

Taking Aim

> [8] *Their horses also are swifter than the leopards, and are more fierce than the evening wolves: and their horsemen shall spread themselves, and their horsemen shall come from far; they shall fly as the eagle that hasteth to eat.*
>
> —Habakkuk 1:8

The Chaldeans (Babylonians) are coming, warns minor prophet Habakkuk in this short book of the Bible, and oh, they are terrible indeed. They'll home in on Judah like an eagle with its eyes locked on its prey.

The eyes of birds of prey are indeed something to be reckoned with. They face forward, not to the sides like those of our friend the robin and many other backyard birds. That gives them true binocular vision, with both eyes working together to bring an object into sharp focus.

Binocular vision also lets them estimate, with pinpoint accuracy, the distance to any object of interest. Very useful when you have to take a mouse or rabbit by surprise.

Seeing like a hawk yet? No?

Well, let's add this: "flicker threshold." No, we're not talking about a woodpecker at the door. We're talking about flickering movement.

Did you know a fluorescent light bulb actually emits flashes of light, not a steady glow? Yeah, me neither, until I started researching bird vision.

Those flashes move at 60 Hertz (Hz). And our lousy eyes can't clearly discern anything that's moving at more than 50 Hz.

Think of it as a movie—our eyes can see 50 images per second, making them appear to our brain as a seamless whole. Speed up the camera to 60 Hz, and we miss part of the action, because our eyes can't keep up. Our flicker threshold is just too low for us to make out individual images.

A flicker faster than 50 Hz, and it's just a blur. Or in the case of that fluorescent light bulb, the illusion of a steady glow.

Not so, to birds of prey. Their flicker threshold is way higher. So, a Cooper's hawk, say, is still seeing every detail, sharp as a tack, when pursuing a bird through the forest.

Just to make you feel even worse, even chickens have us beat. Their flicker threshold is 100 Hz.

And now comes the secret weapon: ultraviolet sight.

Birds of prey not only see things in the good old ROY G. BIV spectrum of the rainbow, like we do. They can also detect ultraviolet light.

See the scent trail of urine droplets that little vole left across your yard? What, you can't see it?

That fruitfly-watching kestrel can. And so can other birds of prey, because the urine reflects ultraviolet light. Nice try at scurrying, little vole, but sayonara, as soon as a hawk gets on your trail.

Finally, the crowning touch: a great pair of sunglasses.

Those would be the prominent ridges above a raptor's eyes, which serve to keep out glare from the sun, as well as shield the eyeballs from dust and wind. Built-in Ray-Bans® are pretty handy for birds who can dive at speeds up to 200 mph.

The Great Speckled Bird

> [9] *Mine heritage is unto me as a speckled bird, the birds round about are against her; come ye, assemble all the beasts of the field, come to devour.*

—Jeremiah 12:9

Yep, it's the King James Version again. And as we now know, "bird" and "birds" may well refer to birds of prey.

And that is exactly how the verse is translated in many other versions of the Bible: either as "birds of prey" or "hawk" in both instances in which the King James Version says "bird(s)."

Birds of prey will indeed turn on one of their own relatives, should the opportunity present itself.

As for that speckled bird, it may well have been the Eurasian sparrowhawk. This smallish accipiter, the Old World counterpart of our sharp-shinned and Cooper's hawks, is definitely speckled on its breast and underside.

"What a Beautiful Thought I Am Thinking..."

"...Concerning a great speckled bird." That's the opening line of a hymn by the Rev. Guy Smith.

Country singer Roy Acuff put it on a record in 1936, for an almost-instant hit. Later, Johnny Cash, Kitty Wells, Jerry Lee Lewis, and, in 1978, Lucinda Williams jumped on the "Great Speckled Bird" bandwagon.

The ending of the song is just as uplifting as we imagine a real live speckled bird's escape might be: "She is spreading her wings for a journey... She'll rise and go up in the sky."

And the Eurasian sparrowhawk is small in size, compared to bulky buteo hawks and to eagles, of which the Bible lands had a big number.

Hard to hold your own when you're the physical underdog, being eyed by bigger, stronger birds of prey.

Yet the threatened hawk—with other birds and beasts drawing closer—had some advantages on his or her side.

These accipiters are swift and agile, built for slaloming at high speed between trees in a forest. And when crossing open spaces, they can dive, climb, twist, and do other aerobatics to evade the clutches of a bigger, slower flier.

Our own American accipiters, the sharp-shinned and Cooper's hawks, share those same skills. Only a few decades ago, they rarely left the woods—they were birds of the forest.

Then came the boom in bird-feeding, which meant easy meals for swift, agile hawks.

How'd they learn about the bounty at feeders?

I'm guessing it had to do with recognizing an opportunity when they saw it.

Many accipiters, including our sharp-shinned (or "sharpie," as these small hawks are often called) and Cooper's hawks, are mi-grants. Apparently, somewhere along the line of those back-and-forth journeys, the birds happened to notice that backyards had become happy hunting grounds, full of juncos, chickadees, and plump doves.

Nowadays, it's rare to go through the winter without hosting an accipiter at the feeder. "Feeder," to those meat-eaters, being not the seeds and suet, but the other birds gathered there to eat.

The writer(s) of this part of the Bible may have meant this passage as an allegory for the Church. But to those who watch birds of prey, it's just an ordinary day in survival-of-the-fittest Nature.

And, judging from the words of song, we know there may well have been a happy ending for the speckled bird.

Clean-up Crew

> [6] *They shall be left together unto the fowls of the mountains, and to the beasts of the earth: and the fowls shall summer upon them, and all the beasts of the earth shall winter upon them.*
>
> —Isaiah 18:6

Bodies. We're talking bodies here. Human bodies. God was in the vineyard, doing some pruning. And letting the, um, "branches" fall where they may.

Oh yeah, King James translators, we know exactly what you're talking about here with the word "fowls." And it ain't chickens. (Which hadn't even been domesticated yet.) It's birds of prey.

As for who's about to get eaten?

> [1] *Woe to the land…which is beyond the rivers of Ethiopia.*
>
> —Isaiah 18:1

No matter. Any body is a good body, as far as vultures and other carrion-eating birds of prey are concerned.

The Body Farm

Hang on to your lurching stomach for this one: In Texas, an outdoor lab, affectionately called the Body Farm, helps forensics investigators learn how to pinpoint the time and causes of human death.

Human bodies—there's a waiting list of donors—are put out in the field to study, with scientists keeping careful track of the arrival of carrion beetles and other critters that help in decomposition.

The Texas "body farm" was the first of these outdoor labs to add vultures to the mix.

And that's where investigators made a major discovery. Via cameras, they watched a flock of vultures descend and go to town. The birds jumped up and down on the body, breaking ribs to make it easier to eat. If a crime victim had been dumped outside, the broken bones might be misinterpreted as perpetrator-caused trauma.

Time of death had to be revamped, too. Before the vultures were factored in, estimated times could be as long as six months or more for a body to become nothing but a skeleton. Thanks to the strong-stomached researchers in Texas, we now know that it might take only two weeks for a fresh body to get down to bone. Vultures are dedicated to their job.

Funneling Through

> [26] *Doth the hawk fly by thy wisdom, and stretch her wings*
> *toward the south?*
>
> —Job 39:26

God does everything, he reminds Job, and in this book of the Bible, he lays it all out, detailing everything that's under his watchful eye and guidance.

And Job knows next to nothing, God reminds him over and over, through the recitation of "Who did this? And this? And this?"

Hawks don't look to Job for guidance when it's time to migrate. Those hawks aren't sitting around waiting for the word "Go!" from a puny human being.

Nope. The birds move when it's time, getting their signals from the things that God created, as he reminds the now utterly humbled Job.

They migrate according to the sun—days getting shorter, for fall migration takeoff; days getting longer, for spring migration.

Which way to go? By landmarks, or by the stars (for birds who fly by night, like barn owls), or, although it's not spelled out in the Bible, by steering a course by sensing the Earth's magnetic field.

Many years ago, before I ever owned my first field guide, I spent a lot of time at Hawk Mountain Sanctuary, a hawk-watching lookout near my home.

Tens of thousands of hawks, eagles, falcons, ospreys (and monarch butterflies) follow the spine of that particular Appalachian ridge as they head south.

Conversation among the handful of dedicated hawk-lovers was sparse back then, but I learned a lot, anyway.

One day, without taking his binoculars from his eyes, the director of the Sanctuary mentioned that he was planning to organize a birdwatching trip to Israel.

"Israel? Why Israel?"

I pictured colorful, exotic birds singing and flying among the—palm trees? jungle vines? cactuses? sand dunes? It may as well have been Mars to someone who was still working on trying to tell one wood warbler from another.

"Raptors," he said, briefly.

"Huh," I answered, astutely. Only years later did I learn that Israel is the Mecca for those who love birds of prey.

Fly Away Home

Israel holds a unique position geographically, as far as migrating birds are concerned. It's part of a funnel.

A funnel that collects birds of prey moving south from the expanse of Europe and Asia, and pours them down into Africa.

> ^{19} *The way of an eagle in the air; the way of a serpent upon a rock; the way of a ship in the midst of the sea; the way of a man with a maid.*

> —Proverbs 30:19

Daytime migrants often depend on the landmarks below to guide them along their journey. Mountain ranges are a common roadmap for many species, including birds of prey.

And when it comes to crossing a wide stretch of water to get from one piece of land to another, migrants often take the same course we would—they look for a bridge.

The Mediterranean Sea is a formidable obstacle. So, for thousands of years, a living river of birds of prey has flown over the land bridge of Israel, Palestine, and northeast Egypt, a valley that's part of the great Syrian-Africa Rift.

Can you picture what a sight that migration must be in a land that's chockfull of raptors?

Streaming overhead, giant vultures and eagles are joined by

chunky buteos ("buzzards," remember?), great numbers of the wasp-eating accipiters called honey-buzzards, plus aerodynamic kites, slim falcons, and other birds of prey of smaller species.

I still haven't seen the spectacle, but I expect it's an unbelievable parade of fantastic birds. Ecotourism operators have taken notice, and nowadays you can book your own personal tour to see the show. The migration keeps on going for weeks, until all of the travelers clear the bottleneck.

The very thought of such a scene gives me sympathy for those Bible translators. With multitudes like this, I would've probably just lumped 'em all together, too.

No Plans for Dinner

[13] *And the glede, and the kite, and the vulture after his kind,*

—Deuteronomy 14:13

"Thou shalt nots," all, as far as eating birds of prey. Deuteronomy and Leviticus spell out the dietary prohibitions, and this time the Bible gets more specific. No gledes. No kites. No vultures.

Fine. I wasn't hungry for them anyhow.

"Glede," by the way, most likely means the red kite. "Kite" alone, the more common black kite.

Not birds that we have here, although perhaps those species of kites that tilt and hover in our skies are equally tasty.

Can't eat them. Not allowed.

> [15] *And the owl, and the night hawk, and the cuckow, and the hawk after his kind,*
>
> —Deuteronomy 14:15

No hawks? But there're so many of them....

No, says God, in no uncertain terms. No hawks of any kind.

Fine.

How about a nice big juicy eagle? Why, that could sustain the whole family for a week! And just think of the size of those drumsticks. Yum!

> [17] *And the pelican, and the gier eagle, and the cormorant,*
>
> —Deuteronomy 14:17

Foiled again. Eagles are off the table, too, even if the King James Version only mentions one type by name. Which is actually a vulture, not an eagle.

We'll just put that down to a translation variation, since other versions of the Bible go with the all-encompassing "eagles" in the list of prohibited menu items.

It's not only those who follow the Bible that leave birds of prey off the dinner table. No culture in the world eats them, or has ever been known to eat them.

The birds may be killed to use feathers, talons, or other parts of them in ceremonies or as adornments. But eaten? Seems like every person under the sun has always said, "No thanks."

BIRDS OF PREY
Eyes in the Sky

American range: Various species of eagles, hawks, falcons, kites, vultures, throughout North America. During migration, various species may appear far from their usual breeding or wintering range.

Natural diet: Raptors vary in their food preferences, but, in general, most depend on animals, birds, reptiles, amphibians, and carrion. For the bald eagle, osprey, and Mississippi kite, it's fish; for the Everglades kite, snails.

At the feeder: Only a few hawk species frequent backyard feeders—in search of your other birds.

American species: At least 30 different species.

Species in the Bible area: At least 50 different species.

A note on translation: It's a confused mess, but the meaning of the Scripture verses is still clear. See earlier sections of this chapter for details.

Chapter 6

Vulture

Nature's Recycler

² For the indignation of the Lord is upon all nations, and his fury upon all their armies: he hath utterly destroyed them, he hath delivered them to the slaughter.

—Isaiah 34:2

Oh boy! It's gonna be a feast!

For vultures, that is.

See any lammergeyers today? How about a griffon? An ossifrage? Gier eagle, perhaps?

All of those are Bible words for vultures. Old World vultures, to be exact.

Which are way different animals than our New World turkey vulture and black vulture.

Unlike our American vultures, Old World species are closely related to eagles. These birds can reach immense size, with wings that stretch nearly 10 feet across.

Only one North American vulture, the very rare California condor, largest American land bird, matches that size.

Only 226 California condors live in the wild, as of May 2012, so count yourself very very lucky to ever lay eyes on one of these magnificent creatures.

Our more-usual species, the turkey vulture and the black vulture, are puny guys by comparison.

They may look big to us, but with a wingspan of 4½ to 6 feet, they're only a little more than half the size of some of the Old World species.

Why, they're practically downright dainty.

In size, that is.

Not so in eating habits.

My, What a Big Nose You Have!

> [3] *Their slain also shall be cast out, and their stink shall come up out of their carcases, and the mountains shall be melted with their blood.*
>
> —Isaiah 2:3

Death and destruction are coming, warned Isaiah in his book, which details the end of the displeasing-to-God kingdom of Judah.

And what a bloodbath it's going to be. The sword of the Lord would be "filled with blood."

You can practically hear the vultures licking their chops.

Dead animals (and in the case of the black vulture, sometimes newborn or otherwise helpless living animals) are the main dish *du jour* for these birds.

Vultures spend a lot of time cruising the skies. You might think they're looking for food.

They are.

But they're also sniffing the air.

Our New World vultures find food both by sight and by smell.

Winner by a Nose

Our black and turkey vultures share one very noticeable physical trait: their noses.

Both species have huge nostrils in the top of their curved beaks. And no septum—look at a vulture beak from the side, and you can see daylight straight through those nose holes.

All the better to smell with.

Our own turkey vulture is the winner in the "biggest nose" category. It even beats out the Andean and California condors and the black vulture, as far as the relative size of its nose. "Nose" being the nostrils or nares, the olfactory chamber, and the olfactory bulb—the organs of smell.

Turkey vultures win by a nose in all three categories.

Like sharks detecting a drop of blood in the sea, they can follow the faintest scent of carrion for miles to home in on the feast.

And their sharp eyes easily detect anything that looks like it might have possibilities, as I found out for myself when I unwittingly conducted an experiment in my garden.

What Smells So Good?

"Frost tonight," warned the forecast one early autumn night.

Oh no, not my tomatoes!

I wasn't ready to say goodbye to homemade BLTs quite yet, so I grabbed the first piece of fabric I found in my "someday I'll make something out of this" pile.

It happened to be a lovely Indian cotton, an abstract print in shades of maroon with bright red and sky-blue accents.

I spread the yardage over my garden, tucking in the big patch of tomatoes under a lumpy lightweight blanket.

Next morning, I hurried outside first thing, to see how the plants had fared.

Whoa! Vultures!

Six of them, standing like hulking children around my tomato patch, cocking their naked heads as they intently examined the fabric. Which, now that I thought about it, was colored exactly the same as dead meat.

Okay. So vultures find food by sight.

Um, not so fast.

About a month later, I was mowing the overgrown meadow when I accidentally hit a nest of baby cottontail rabbits. To my horror, one was already dead before I could yank the mower backward. Feeling terrible, I covered the tiny body with long dry grass, to rest in eternal peace.

The weather was unusually warm that year, and within a day or so, my nose caught the faintest whiff of carrion.

"I'm sorry, bunny," I whispered.

Then I noticed that somebody else had picked up on the distinctive aroma. Two somebodies.

A pair of turkey vultures were overhead, circling in tighter and tighter loops, as they zeroed in on the exact spot that "delicious" smell was coming from.

Hidden in the house, I watched them drop to the prey. In minutes, that baby bunny was in their bellies.

Being able to find food by both sight and scent is a big help to the birds in our varied landscape. Some carrion may be right out in the open, but trees and other vegetation keep a lot of possible meals hidden from overhead view.

Old World vultures, say scientists, lack the keen sense of smell of our New World guys. Luckily, big areas of their range are wide-open deserts or plains, where it's easy to find food by sight alone.

Sniff, Sniff

When natural gas companies added foul-smelling ethyl mercaptan to the odorless gas in order to make any leaks by gas furnaces or appliances instantly obvious to the nose, they discovered another benefit.

Turkey vultures gathered around certain parts of the pipelines. Parts where the pipes had sprung a leak. The odor smelled like carrion to the birds, and they were hoping they'd find food.

Nice early warning system. When vultures gather, workers go to check it out: Could be a dead animal. But might be a gas leak.

Keep Your Cool

Vultures use their hooked bills to strip meat, cleaning off all the fat and muscles and tendons, right down to the bone.

But they also stick their heads and necks deep into the body, to get at the good parts.

And that's where a bald head comes in handy. Or so you would think. Easier to keep clean, of course.

Maybe not.

Look at the head of a turkey vulture or black vulture. It's not smooth and taut, like the bald dome of Mr. Clean® of housekeeping-products fame.

Instead, the skin is wrinkled, laying in folds like a sock that's lost its elastic, or pebbled like pigskin. Lots of nooks and crannies for blood and guts to accumulate.

And many Old World vultures have feathered heads. Granted, the feathers are fine, almost plush-like, but still, they're feathers.

So what's the deal?

Hats. And lack thereof. Or, as scientists call it, *thermoregulation*.

Vultures of all species have to be able to tolerate big swings in temperature.

Desert air may be baking hot—some areas of the Middle East hit 125°F—down at ground level.

But at the altitudes where the birds soar, or on the cliffs on which they perch, the temperature is colder than on a sun-baked valley floor.

Soaking up the Sun

In the morning, or when the sun comes out after a rain, vultures often spread their wings to warm up. They relax their shoulders and bend their elbows and wrists, drooping their wings and letting them splay outward.

It's quite a sight to see the big birds perched with their "laundry" on the line. They turn to face the sun, open those magnificent pinions, and let them soak up the warmth for as little as a minute or as long as a quarter-hour.

Preening, scratching, and shaking their heads often accompanies the morning wakeup, which looks an awful lot like any animal—including us and our dogs and cats—waking up from a nap.

Swinging back and forth between hot and cold is just a normal part of life for any vulture.

So they need a way to regulate their own temperature, in order to stay comfortable.

And now we come to what scientists say is the real reason for that bald head.

Dark skin—red or dark grayish black, in the case of our New World species, as well as Old World birds—absorbs heat.

Folds and wrinkles help hang on to that warmth, just as they do on our own bodies. (Just think about where you sweat first, and most—the creases of knees, the armpits, and other places where skin meets skin.)

In ultra-hot conditions, air currents quickly cool that bare skin, especially when the bird stretches out its head and neck to eliminate the heat-holding folds. The short-feathered heads and necks of Old World species, same effect.

In colder temps, a vulture draws its head back into its shoulders, snuggling the bare skin in feathers as it hunches up.

Really, really cold? Draw that head in even further, until only the beak is exposed.

Meanwhile, Mr. Clean® of TV-commercial fame has to reach for his hat when the chill sets in. And take it off when he's out mowing the lawn in the dog days of August.

Cast-Iron Stomach

¹⁴ *And the vulture, and the kite after his kind;*

—Leviticus 11:14

Vultures are just one more animal in a long line of food prohibitions, spelled out in both Leviticus and Deuteronomy.

Not that we look at these big birds with a hungry eye.

Maybe we've learned and remember the Bible warnings, or similar prohibitions in other religious texts.

Maybe it's because of our cultural eating habits, which cause us to never even consider trying vulture meat as our newest gourmet adventure. Chicken, yes. Vulture, no.

Or maybe it's an innate or even instinctive taboo, born from the knowledge that these birds are foul, not fowl.

For whatever reason, it's no wonder vultures don't make it to the dinner table.

Never have, and most likely never will.

Why doesn't the thought of eating a big, meaty vulture make us go "Yum"?

Well, because doing so could kill us, for one thing.

These birds are living reservoirs of deadly bacteria. Much of the carrion they eat has died of infectious diseases, or carries those dangerous germs.

In studies, the big birds of prey have been shown to be serving as a living home to a full baker's dozen of pathogens.

Any one of which could lay us low.

Really low. As in, dead.

No problem to vultures, though. Immune to the germs, the birds remain hale and hearty, enjoying good health while chowing down on bad food.

We, on the other hand, grasp our bellies in pain when we get even a slight taste of *Escherichia coli* (*E. coli*, as we know it), *Enterobacter*, *Clostridium botulinum* (botulism), *Salmonella*, and other bacterial baddies that a vulture's stomach can harbor without a qualm.

How do the birds do it? Somehow, like corvids and other critters on the "do not eat" list, their own bodies manage to manufacture antibodies to the pathogens.

Neat trick! And one that we humans can't do. So, sorry, no taking a bite out of these birds of prey.

Making a Vee Line

> [4] *Thou shalt exalt thyself as the eagle, and though thou set thy nest among the stars, thence will I bring thee down, saith the Lord.*
>
> —Obadiah 1:4

The shortest book in the Bible, Obadiah has only one chapter, but it's a doozy. It's a vision of the destruction of the kingdom of Idumea (or Edom), south of Judah, concurring with prophecies by other Bible prophets.

And it's a lesson, in some parts, about pride.

Unfounded pride.

Which is why I always think of an old, now-dead acquaintance when I read that line. A self-appointed "mystic" of sorts, he took great pride in pointing out eagles to other people.

Usually, the eagles he spotted came sailing by in pairs, or trios, or groups.

"A good omen!" he'd declare, gazing raptly and reverently at the big birds soaring and circling overhead.

Then, proudly, he'd add, "Eagles always come to me." The unstated subtext being, "because I'm special, and you're not."

Only one problem: Every time, he was pointing to vultures, not eagles.

Had he known, I have a feeling he wouldn't have been so quick to claim credit.

"V for Vulture"

I didn't bother correcting the guy who saw "eagles" everywhere. So they weren't eagles, so what? I love vultures just as much as eagles. To me, they're just as worthy of respect. And just as beautiful. And even more fun to watch, especially when they're flying.

But if I noticed a dissenting murmur from any doubting Thomases in his audience, I did quietly pass along a quick tip:

"Just remember, *'V for Vulture.'* Vultures fly with their wings held up in a wide V. Eagles, wings straight across."

That mnemonic—"V for Vulture"—is a great place to start, when you're trying to identify big birds of prey in North America.

But there are some exceptions.

- Black vultures usually hold their wings flat, not in a V.
- Eagles, on occasion, may angle their wings.
- Some big hawks, including the Swainson's and the rough-legged, adopt the V-shape as their usual mode of going.

But "V for Vulture" is still a pretty safe bet.

Turkey vultures are our most common American species, and they're way more numerous than the V-flying hawks. So a V-winged bird has a pretty good chance of being a vulture.

A group of V wings? Even more likely to be vultures. The V-winged hawks rarely if ever go about in groups.

The V, also called a *dihedral,* has a purpose. It allows the vultures to coast along in their typical "teetering" style, rocking back and forth relatively low to the ground, which improves their chances of picking up the scent of carrion.

The Old World vultures of the Bible lands depend mainly on their sense of sight to find food. So they don't fly like our carrion-sniffers do.

Instead, they hold their wings flat, all the better for steady soaring while peering at the ground, trying to spot their next meal.

Don't Go There

> [15] *There shall the great owl make her nest, and lay, and hatch,*
> *and gather under her shadow: there shall the vultures also be*
> *gathered, every one with her mate.*
>
> —Isaiah 34:15

What else do we need to make us shudder, in Isaiah's vision of God's destruction soon to come onto Judah? Well, only the creepiest of birds will be around.

Abandon hope, all ye that might've thought about entering. Ain't nobody home but just us owls and vultures.

And Isaiah was right, in his forecast of the birds to be found, and in evoking a scene of desolation.

At nesting time, vultures seek isolation.

The big birds may roost or feed around our towns, roads, and houses—wherever there's yummy dead food to be found.

But when it's time to raise a family, away they go, to the far ends of the earth. Or at least some miles away from the interruption of our comings and goings.

Vultures are cavity-nesting birds. But don't even think about trying to build them a birdhouse.

We're talking a cavity on the grand scale.

It has to be someplace the birds can crawl into from an opening. A cave, a crevice in rock outcroppings or cliffs, a hollow tree, stump, or a big hollow log on the ground—all may serve as home sweet home to a happy pair of vultures.

Whichever site the vulture couple chooses, two openings into the cavity are preferred, so there's an escape route if need be.

In the American West, nest sites in rocks win by a mile: almost 9 out of 10 nests.

In the East, variety is the name of the game. Vultures there nest in rocks, in dead stumps, in hollow trees (sycamores are a favorite), in logs. Any secret place is a good place to hole up.

Oh—and there is no nest, per se.

Vultures lay their two eggs right on the surface of whatever's inside that hole. Rotted wood, bits of straw or other debris, pebbles, bare earth? To a vulture, all good. Home decor just doesn't matter, as long as the family is safely out of sight.

Sub-Letted Structures

As long as no human activity is going on nearby, vultures may nest in our own deserted structures—hunting blinds, haylofts, dilapidated houses, a chimney of an abandoned house or factory.

As for Isaiah's disturbing scene of wrack and ruin?

On a smaller scale, one of the most chilling sights to me is a chimney still standing where a house burned down to the ground.

When I happened upon such a chimney one day and heard loud hisses and grunts emanating from inside it…well, yes, creepy was the only word for it.

It took a minute before I connected the dots: Vultures and vulture babies hiss when they feel threatened, and this chimney was their home.

I withdrew and waited patiently.

Before long, a naked head with beady eye slowly cleared the top of the chimney like a periscope. Yep. Vulture home.

Instantly, the creepy feeling disappeared. Oh boy, vultures! Cool!

Cuddle Up

Our North American vultures are much more inclined to share our company than the massive birds of the Middle East, which truly do live in desolate places—crags and cliffs and mountain forests.

Oh sure, our birds may also retreat to such sites when it's nesting time.

But most of the year, home is where the heart—er, food—is. And that means close to human habitation.

Turkey and black vultures both roost communally. Dozens, scores, sometimes even thousands of birds settle for the night in the same place, often in mixed company with each other.

Every evening, the birds return to their chosen rest site. In the morning, they disperse to go a-hunting.

The biggest roost sites ever inventoried in the U.S. are in Florida. One sleeping spot at Lake Okeechobee held 4,000 vultures in wintertime. No need to hang a "Do Not Disturb" sign—I doubt that anyone except scientists with counting gadgets are heading for that resting spot.

Yep, our vultures are sociable critters.

Sleeping in close company, flying in flocks all day, sharing the "dinner table" around that dead animal, it's a wonderfully social life, day in and day out.

Then comes nesting time.

And now things change.

Like a honeymooning couple, a pair of vultures isn't shy about saying, "Hey, we need a little space here."

When it's time to set up housekeeping, the birds spread out, with each couple having its own backyard. Usually at least a half-mile away from its closest vulture neighbors, according to some studies of vulture-preferred real estate.

Lasting Digs

No shopping for a new home every spring: Vultures re-use the same nest sites year after year. While no banding research has been done, plenty of observations—including my own—show that vultures return to use the same crack in the rock, hollow log, or other home the next year, and the next, and the next.

Are they the same pair? No way to know. But since turkey and black vultures can live 15 years or more, they may well be.

Nesting starts early for vultures, usually in February or March. If you spot these big birds entering or exiting a crevice or other likely nest site, you can enjoy weeks of spying on the family with binoculars. Plus a good chance of doing it all over again next year.

Tourist Trap

[7] There is a path which no fowl knoweth, and which the vulture's eye hath not seen.

—Job 28:7

Carrion-eating birds of prey may not be quite as romantic as, say, the swallows of Capistrano. But their return is just as regular as those clockwork swallows. And some communities have managed to turn their vultures into a money-making opportunity.

March 15 is the red-letter day for Hinckley, Ohio.

That's when the vultures return to "Buzzard's Roost" in the Hinckley Reservation, administered by Cleveland Metroparks.

It's a lovely area, and one that is sometimes chosen as a honeymoon spot. But a pair of newlyweds I ran into years ago told me their experience at the Hinckley park wasn't quite the peaceful retreat they'd envisioned for their honeymoon.

Seems the way to call in the vultures is by shooting guns at daybreak. It's a dinner bell of sorts to the carrion-eating birds. They've learned to associate the sound of a gun with the enticing thought of possible leftovers.

But the newlywed couple was good-natured and loved birds. They were happy to share the occasion with migrating vultures.

Besides, the return of the vultures is a big day for Hinckley. The visitors' center sells buzzard souvenirs, people take pride in spotting the first of the new arrivals, and there's a full-blown festival, proudly proclaimed "Buzzards Day."

Only problem? As with many other bird species, including those famed Capistrano swallows, vulture migration habits are shifting in response to climate change.

Hinckley's vultures had been returning on about the same date since 1957, but in recent years, they're coming back earlier. No word on whether the town will change the date of its welcome-home party.

Other towns aren't so quick to celebrate their status as a destination for big numbers of carrion-eaters. In fact, some towns
adopted by big flocks of vultures would prefer no one to know.

Secret path? You bet. And let's keep it that way.

But unlike the path in Job 28:7, these routes are well known to
the eyes of vultures.

The Secret Attraction

It was a fine spring day when I drove to Santa Claus, Indiana, to
give a talk to the local garden club. Home to "Holiday World," a
Christmas-themed amusement park, the whole town seemed as
unnaturally tidy (unnaturally to me, anyway) as Disneyland.

Lawns of perfect green velvet. Gleaming cars. Not a weed in
any garden. No piles of junk in backyards. Windows and door-
frames, spiffy with new paint…and what in the world were those
big white splashes on the roofs?!

Vulture excrement, that's what. Liquid droppings, ejected with
force by perching birds.

Forget the garden gnomes and other doodads in the tidy
yards—now this was a decoration you don't see every day!

The turkey vultures themselves sat hulking on many a roof.
And on the neat-as-a-pin lawns. And on flagpoles and street lights.

Quite the contrast.

"I had no idea you had so many vultures! They're all over, and
so tame," I started my speech, raving about the birds.

An instant, disapproving "Shhhh!" went around the room.

"We don't talk about them," a woman muttered.

Fine. I yanked myself back to the gardening topic.

But for me, Santa Claus, Indiana, will always be "the place
with the vultures," not "the place with the amusement park."

I like secret paths. Especially when I get to share them with an
incongruous bunch of hulking vultures.

VULTURE
Turkey Vulture (*Cathartes aura*)
Black Vulture (*Coragyps atratus*)
California Condor (*Gymnogyps californianus*)

American range: Turkey vulture, all across the country; black vulture, mostly in the Southeast. California condor, mainly California; also parts of Arizona and Utah; also re-introduced to Grand Canyon area.

Natural diet: Carrion.

At the feeder: Uh, got any roadkill in the fridge? Big roadkill?

American species: 3 species of New World vultures: turkey vulture, black vulture, and the rare California condor.

Species in the Bible area: At least 5 species of Old World vultures.

A note on translation: Various versions of the Bible differ in translation when it comes to the word "vulture." In this chapter, I've used verses from the King James Version that, to me, seem to be clearly referring to vultures. See Chapter 5, Birds of Prey, for more details on differences of opinion in translation.

Chapter 7

Eagle
Wings of Awe

14 And to the woman were given two wings of a great eagle, that she might fly into the wilderness, into her place, where she is nourished for a time, and times, and half a time, from the face of the serpent.

—Revelation 12:14

It takes patience to appreciate eagles.

Oh, I'm not talking about at first sight.

That's always a special moment—"Oh boy, an EAGLE!"—whether the big bird is soaring overhead or perched and watching.

But waiting for an eagle to actually *do* something, well, that's a different story.

It may be an hour before the bird leaves its perch.

Two hours before a bald eagle dives at a flock of ducks.

Four hours before it comes up with a fish.

And that's only if you happen to be in the right place at the right time.

Golden eagles are just as sedentary. In one study, male golden eagles spent 78% of daylight hours sitting on a perch. Females were even less active—they were perched 85% of the time.

Eagle time is patience personified. Go into it knowing that, and you won't get antsy. And you may eventually get to see something that takes your breath away.

Homes on High

> ²⁷ *Doth the eagle mount up at thy command, and make her nest on high?*

>   —Job 39:27

God was speaking here. Reminding Job—who had a little problem with pride—that it wasn't a lowly human who was in charge. Of the whole world. And everything in it.

It's not our doing, either.

But boy oh boy, what fun to see those wonders around us. Especially eagles, nesting on high.

The eagles of the Middle East, all 10 or more species, may well make their homes only on the most remote cliffs. I've never been there, so I can't say. But it's a reasonable assertion, because these giant birds like an eagle's-eye view.

> ¹⁶ *Thy terribleness hath deceived thee, and the pride of thine heart, O thou that dwellest in the clefts of the rock, that holdest the height of the hill: though thou shouldest make thy nest as high as the eagle, I will bring thee down from thence, saith the Lord.*

>   —Jeremiah 49:16

No hiding from God. Pride goeth before a fall, we well know.

One of our own American eagles has come down to lesser heights of its own accord. Instead of nesting only far, far away from human activity, way up on the tallest cliff around, our bald eagles build their immense bowls of sticks in trees, on utility poles, or on raised platforms near docks, fishing holes, and other places we people frequent.

Our golden eagles, though, are still birds of wild country. Maybe that's why a sighting of one of these birds with its gleaming blonde head is even more of a thrill than spotting the white-headed symbol of our country.

Golden eagles are only occasionally seen in the eastern half of the country. But in the West, with its rodent-rich habitat, any outing may include a golden sighting. It's worth keeping your eyes open, and taking a second look at any big dark bird when you're west of the Plains.

Naked as a Vulture

Make thee bald, and poll thee for thy delicate children; enlarge thy baldness as the eagle; for they are gone into captivity from thee.
—Micah 1:16

Jacob had transgressed. The House of Israel had strayed. Get ready, said Micah—God is coming to deliver your punishment. And you'll be sorry. In fact, you should shave your head, as a sign of mourning.

Micah wasn't talking about our bald eagle here, and I doubt he was referring to any white-headed eagle of Bible lands.

Although our national symbol bears the moniker "bald," its head is definitely well-feathered.

"Make thee bald" means no feathers at all.

A naked head? That's a trait that no eagle exhibits.

I think Micah was evoking vultures—which, as you may recall, were as big as eagles in those regions, and so similar in flight, they were hard to distinguish (see Chapter 5, Birds of Prey, for more details on translation).

What's on the Menu?

¹⁹ *Our persecutors are swifter than the eagles of the heaven: they pursued us upon the mountains, they laid wait for us in the wilderness.*

—Lamentations 4:19

Lamenting the destruction of Jerusalem, including the Holy Temple, this book of the Bible notes that the enemies pursued the fleeing people like eagles, into all sorts of difficult terrain.

Real eagles live in the same sorts of places and are just as far-ranging, traveling swiftly through wilderness and waterways.

Our bald eagle belongs to the group called *sea eagles*. They have an affinity for water, although you'll also see them far from lakes and rivers. Bald eagles eat mainly fish, but they dine on ducks and other waterfowl, too, as well as land animals.

Golden eagles aren't sea eagles. They mainly patrol the land, not the waters. Although golden eagles are big enough and strong enough to nab a hefty lamb or even a sheep, their diet is mainly small animals, not large ones. And definitely not fish.

Small animals make up the bulk of a golden's diet in the American West. Rabbits are #1, followed by prairie dogs, ground squirrels, and other rodents. Keep in mind that the jackrabbits of the West aren't little bunnies—they can reach 2 feet long and weigh a solid 6 pounds.

Most of these animals scoot fast into burrows to escape an eagle's clutches, and those that live in colonies post a lookout to keep an eye on the skies.

Rarely do any of them stray far from a quick escape hatch—a hole to a burrow, even if it belongs to a neighbor and not to the animal itself. Or the protective cover of a bush or clump of grass.

So the eagle uses a low flight to take them by surprise.

Called *contour flight*, this route follows the lay of the land, skimming low over sagebrush, rising a bit to clear outcroppings of rock. Watching a golden hunt in this manner is like seeing a topographical map come to life as the big bird skims just a few feet from the ground, dipping and rising along with the land.

Golden eagles do hunt mid-sized and large animals, too. Goats, sheep, lambs, antelopes, ibex (the golden eagle is a worldwide species), and foxes fall into the eagle-food category.

Second to animals on the golden's menu are birds. Grouse, cranes, swans—all fair game, along with everything in between.

Good News!

Nowadays, you don't have to travel to Alaska or British Columbia—the last bastions of good numbers of bald eagles, as recently as 20 years ago—to lay your eyes on the symbol of our country.

Bald eagles are one of the big conservation success stories in the United States. Although their numbers sank abysmally low by 1980, they've come roaring back. In August, 2007, the bald eagle was removed from the U.S. Endangered Species List.

You have a good chance of spotting an awesome bald eagle near any body of water in the country, from the Atlantic and Pacific shores, to the Great Lakes and major rivers, to any local creek or pond that's big enough to hold fish or ducks. Enjoy!

Watch for Whitewash

One of the best ways to spot a golden eagle? Look for white streaks on cliffs, especially at nesting time—those are the splashes of droppings from big birds, which squirt rather than plop.

It may be a raven nest site. Might be vultures. But it could be an eagle home. And if the golden pair chose to raise their family in that area, you may spot them even in the off season, sitting on the cliff or scouring the skies.

A Devoted Couple

[11] *As an eagle stirreth up her nest, fluttereth over her young,*
  spreadeth abroad her wings, taketh them, beareth them on her
  wings:

—Deuteronomy 32:11

I'm thinking it should be eagles rather than doves that serve as a symbol of enduring love.

Like doves, eagles mate for life, with no fooling around on the side allowed. But unlike short-lived doves, which barely last a year or two in the wild, eagles are the oldtimers of the bird world.

These birds may live as long as 30 years, and, in much of the country, the happy couple stays together year-round throughout their lifetime.

Now that's a symbol worth putting on Valentines and anniversary cards. Even if eagles aren't exactly sweet and cuddly-looking.

Eagles are just as devoted as doves, but they're not nearly as prolific. Bald and golden eagles only raise about 15 young in their whole life.

A nest holds one, possibly two, babies, no matter how many eggs are laid. And the pair may not nest every year: One study

noted that nearly half of the pairs surveyed did not nest in any giv-
en year.

Plus, eagles are late bloomers: Young birds need 3 to 5 years to
grow to maturity and start their own family.

As for that tender behavior described in the Deuteronomy
quote above, yes, eagles are attentive parents. The female doesn't
flutter—that's not something eagles can manage with those gigantic wings—but she does stay close. And she "spreadeth abroad her
wings" to keep the babies shaded from sun or shielded from rain.

But when it's time to leave the nest, those youngsters are on
their own. No hitching a ride on Mom's wings; they have to learn
to use their own.

And that takes practice. Young eagles flap down from the nest
for their first flight. But on subsequent attempts, they often walk
uphill to make it easier to get airborne by aiming down a slope,
until their muscles are strong enough for takeoff.

Family Planning

Rabbits, ground squirrels, and other golden eagle staples run in cy-
cles, building their numbers over a period of several years, then
crashing to scarcity, before the cycle begins to build again.

When prey is hard to come by, golden eagles may not nest at
all during that year.

In areas of the West where the black-tailed jackrabbit lives, the
nesting of golden eagles is closely tied to the breeding success of
the rabbits.

Like other rabbit species, jackrabbits adjust the size of their
brood to the amount of available food and weather conditions.

When the bunnies are abundant, so are eagle chicks.

Bad year for rabbits? Bad year for the eagles that eat them.

Awesome Wings

> *³ And say, Thus saith the Lord God; A great eagle with great*
> *wings, longwinged, full of feathers, which had divers colours,*
> *came unto Lebanon, and took the highest branch of the cedar:*
>
> —Ezekiel 17:3
>
> *⁷ There was also another great eagle with great wings and many*
> *feathers: and, behold, this vine did bend her roots to him, and*
> *shot forth her branches toward him, that he might water it by*
> *the furrows of her plantation.*
>
> —Ezekiel 17:7

This is just part of a lengthy riddle that, according to the prophet Ezekiel, God told him to put to the house of Israel.

The house of Israel, which had broken a covenant. Uh-oh.

In the riddle, the eagle plants the cedar branch in a city of merchants, and plants a seed as well, that turns into a vine, and is watered by another eagle with great wings, and.... Now it's starting to sound like one of my own dreams, full of mixed-up symbolism that by morning vanishes with the first cup of coffee.

We'll get to that caretaking great eagle with its many feathers in a bit. But first, let's take a closer look at the multicolored eagle.

All eagles are some variation on a white/brown/black theme. No blue eagles. No yellow eagles. No red eagles. Nope, just neutral colors, arranged in various patterns.

So "divers[e] colours" could have referred to just about any of the eagles of Bible lands.

Must've been a wonderful bird, no matter what variation of white, brown, or black it was wearing. A set of basic clothes can be pretty stunning. (Hard to beat a dark suit with a white shirt.)

Think of our own bald eagle, with its gleaming white head and tail and somber dark brown body. A stunning creature.

Likewise, our golden eagle.

Shared Glory

Our golden eagle (*Aquila chrysaetos*) isn't only "our" eagle.

He's the Middle East's eagle, too, and soars over Europe, Asia, and parts of Africa. Yep, those wings spread wide, indeed.

With a nesting territory that averages about 60 square miles, these big birds aren't numerous. But they are fairly common, as eagles go, and the species is definitely widespread.

Dressed mostly in plain dark brown, this bird sports gleaming blonde tips on the feathers of its brown head and neck. The effect? Just as eyecatching as a $200 highlighting job from a hair salon.

But who needs feathers of many colors when you've got flying equipment like an eagle's?

It's those great wings that strike awe, whether they're in a Biblical riddle (a veiled allusion to the doom that would soon strike Israel if they didn't straighten up and—sorry—fly right), or in the sky over our own heads.

Or, for that matter, in our dreams and visions. Where they're pretty hard to mistake as anything other than a symbol of strength, power, and stamina.

Eagle #2 in the riddle may have been great indeed, but even its great wings and watering duties couldn't save the fruiting vine. Like somebody who can't resist giving away the answer, God tells Ezekiel to pass this message along:

> [9] *Say thou, Thus saith the Lord God; Shall it prosper? shall he not pull up the roots thereof, and cut off the fruit thereof, that it wither? it shall wither in all the leaves of her spring, even without great power or many people to pluck it up by the roots thereof.*

*10 Yea, behold, being planted, shall it prosper? shall it not
utterly wither, when the east wind toucheth it? it shall wither
in the furrows where it grew.*

—Ezekiel 17:9-10

And then the book of Ezekiel spells out the symbolism.

The first eagle is Nebuchadnezzar, the king of Babylon.

The vine is the kingdom of Judah, which had sworn loyalty to
Babylon.

The second eagle, the one who watered the vine, is Egypt, from
which the king of Judah was seeking help to get out from under
the thumb of Nebuchadnezzar.

Not so fast, King Zedekiah of Judah—you made a promise to
Babylon. And now you've broken it. Punishment will be as swift
and sure as an eagle, says God. Consider yourself warned.

A Bone-Crushing Handshake

> [33] *The same hour was the thing fulfilled upon Nebuchadnezzar: and he was driven from men, and did eat grass as oxen, and his body was wet with the dew of heaven, till his hairs were grown like eagles' feathers, and his nails like birds' claws.*

> —Daniel 4:33

Daniel recounts a disturbing vision to King Nebuchadnezzar—a vision in which the king is the main player.

You will go mad, says Daniel, and live as a beast for seven years. But, oh, what fine feathers and claws you will have!

Claws, eh? Time for a look at some super-duper claws—the feet of eagles.

Let's say you've been practicing for the thumb-wrestling competition. Or maybe you just want to squeeze someone's hand into jelly, next time you shake.

Ready, set, squeeze!

You're exerting a force of about 20 or so pounds per square inch, if you have a grip of average strength. Maybe, with training, you can nudge the number up a bit. If you're a bodybuilder, your grip might approach 50 or even 100 psi.

You're still nowhere near the strength of an eagle's "handshake."

Estimates of the force of those talons are all over the map. They're not even estimates, as far as I can tell, but guesses, since no one has yet figured out how to measure the incredible strength of those claws.

I suppose it wouldn't be easy, getting an eagle to perform on command, nor figuring out how to devise an experiment that would result in an accurate reading.

What we do know is that an eagle's talons can pierce right through a falconer's stoutest glove.

And we know that these birds drive their claws in right up to the hilt, when they're striking prey. Not only do the claws pierce through flesh and organs, they squeeze together like a nightmarish pair of pliers.

Those deadly talons, coupled with the power of the eagle's strong leg muscles and tendons, exert a force that can kill a full-size goat almost instantly.

For a bird that weighs only 5 to 9 pounds, that's not bad.

Who are we kidding? That's incredible!

> [1] *Set the trumpet to thy mouth. He shall come as an eagle against the house of the Lord, because they have transgressed my covenant, and trespassed against my law.*
>
> —Hosea 8:1

Now, that's not a very comforting image. No one wants to be in the crosshairs of an eagle's eyes.

Nothing escapes alive once an eagle gets a grip.

Often, the death squeeze breaks the animal's neck almost instantly. When the prey is a big animal—hopefully not us—death may not be so swift.

Eagles don't prey on people, but they do attack bighorn sheep, mountain goats, and other hefty critters. And that's where a secure grip is vital.

An eagle's leg tendons work as ratchets, interlocking with ridges on the tendon sheaths as they tighten the talons bit by bit. Once an eagle has a grip, the bird can maintain the force without tiring its muscles.

Bad news for prey.

Bad news for anyone reading Hosea's warning, and knowing the damage an eagle can do.

Time to bulk up to defend yourself?

Pleased to meet y—*OUCH!* But, sorry, you're still no match for an eagle's "handshake."

On the Wings of Eagles

> [13] *Behold, he shall come up as clouds, and his chariots shall be as a whirlwind: his horses are swifter than eagles. Woe unto us! for we are spoiled.*
>
> —Jeremiah 4:13

Is it any wonder that most of the Scriptural references to eagles allude to their flight? These are the biggest land birds in the sky (except for some Old World vultures, and our New World condors).

Impossible to overlook.

Eagles fly with flat-out wings, the tips of their feathers winnowing the air to make subtle adjustments to their flight like the ailerons on an airplane's wing.

And what wings they are.

> [40] *For thus saith the Lord; Behold, he shall fly as an eagle, and shall spread his wings over Moab.*
>
> —Jeremiah 48:40

Stretching up to 8 feet from wingtip to wingtip in the bald eagle, and up to 7 feet and change in the golden eagle, the wings are broad as well as long. Those magnificent appendages are built for soaring, something that eagles do *par excellence.*

> [31] *But they that wait upon the Lord shall renew their strength; they shall mount up with wings as eagles; they shall run, and not be weary; and they shall walk, and not faint.*
>
> —Isaiah 40:31

Weary? That word isn't in an eagle's vocabulary. Eagles can spend hours aloft, riding the wind with nary a flap.

Look at the wingtips with binoculars, and you'll see that the feathers spread like the fingers of a hand, each strong pinion making delicate adjustments as needed to keep the eagle on track.

When eagles migrate, leaving the coldest parts of their range for the better opportunities available southward in winter, they can easily travel hundreds of miles in a day.

Set the course, spread the wings, and there you go, sailing to Jerusalem. Or, for our two species, maybe Delaware or California.

Tired? Not at all, thanks!

> [22] *Behold, he shall come up and fly as the eagle, and spread his wings over Bozrah: and at that day shall the heart of the mighty men of Edom be as the heart of a woman in her pangs.*
>
> —Jeremiah 49:22

Hunting is usually done from the sky, although occasionally an eagle will survey the situation from a perch, then, if things look promising, make a gliding dive.

These giant birds are incredibly speedy.

They're also remarkably agile, considering their size.

It's worth the long, patient wait it may require to see an eagle doing something other than perching or soaring. Because their flight is nothing short of jaw-dropping.

Eagles can maneuver those big wings as skillfully as a fighter pilot, skimming low over the ground, twisting and turning on the track of a desperately fleeing animal, or doing aerobatics together as part of their courtship maneuvers.

Down to Earth

In the sky, eagles are the very picture of power, as well as grace and beauty—just as they're symbolically used in the Bible.

> [5] *Wilt thou set thine eyes upon that which is not? For riches certainly make themselves wings; they fly away as an eagle toward heaven.*
>
> —Proverbs 23:5

Riches are transitory; eagles can vanish in a flash, too.

But whenever these big birds are literally down to earth, it's a different story. Eagle landings can be bumpy jobs, even with those great feathered brakes applied.

Once on the ground, eagles are definitely earthbound creatures. All that grace in the air disappears as the bulky bird staggers on its relatively short legs, trying to catch its balance after landing.

Watch an eagle lurch into a run, trying to chase down prey that was missed on the initial strike, and the word "elegant" is hardly the first one that comes to mind.

And takeoff is, as you might expect, a not quite graceful proposition. It takes a lot of effort to get that hefty body airborne, so eagles usually employ a running or hopping start, accompanied by determined flapping of their strong wings.

And that's when they have nothing in their talons. After a successful prey strike, it's even harder for eagles to get back into the air, especially when that meal-to-be is a big one.

Often, the captured animal is eaten right on the spot.

But if the bird needs to feed a nest, it's take-out time, and those doggie bags can carry quite a bit of weight.

That's why eagles often time their strikes so that they don't have to come to a full stop, or alight. Their terrible talons reach out and snag the prey on the fly, so the eagle doesn't lose all of its precious momentum.

Once aloft, the currents of warm air rising from a slope (*thermals*) take the bird back up to soaring level. Again, the epitome of grace and the symbol of strength, heading for the heavens.

Counting Our Gold

> [26] *They are passed away as the swift ships: as the eagle that hasteth to the prey.*
>
> —Job 9:26

Eagles can disappear from sight in just seconds, thanks to their incredible flying ability. And in a larger sense, they can also disappear from sight in a more permanent way.

Bald eagles grabbed the spotlight when their numbers dropped precariously, becoming the focus of dedicated efforts by biologists and volunteers to find and count them.

Not so easy to tally up golden eagles. Most live in remote areas of the West—places not included in the areas inventoried during the annual Christmas Bird Count or in breeding bird surveys.

The Eagle Morgue

Used in religious ceremonies and as honored adornments, eagle feathers are revered as sacred objects by Native Americans of the U.S. (and the First Nations people of Canada).

When the federal Bald and Golden Eagle Protection Act was passed in 1940, possessing any part of the bird became a federal offense, punishable by a fine of up to $25,000. (Unfortunately, it was poorly enforced for years.)

Killing eagles was banned, even on reservations, where it had been a traditional way of garnering feathers. Not a good solution for the many people who needed feathers for their ceremonies.

Eagle feathers had to be supplied in a way that wouldn't further endanger the species. So the government set up the National Eagle Repository, a place to gather all of the bodies of eagles that meet their deaths through hitting utility wires, cars, or in other accidents, as well as victims of poaching.

Persons certified as tribal members can apply for feathers or other parts of the birds. When the request is fulfilled, a permit of legal possession comes along with it, so that the recipient doesn't need to worry about the swift arm of the law swooping down on them like an eagle.

Plus, an eagle easily covers many miles during a day's flight. So it's impossible to say whether that golden eagle we saw this morning in Colorado is the same bird, or a different one, as the eagle our friends in Wyoming saw later that day.

No one knows how many golden eagles grace North America. Best guess? About 70,000 in the U.S. But it's very much a guess.

What ornithologists *have* noted is that the species is declining in the eastern half of the country, where habitat is compromised.

In the West, wildfires—which are increasing in size and frequency, due to the droughts engendered by climate change—have been noted to take a toll, decimating the jackrabbits and other prey animals the eagles depend upon.

But the biggest killer of golden eagles? Us.

Collisions with cars, power lines, and other structures are the leading cause of death. In the winter of 1984–1985 alone, nearly 1,000 golden eagles were killed by cars in Wyoming.

Electrocution, caused when an eagle lands on live power lines or poles, used to be a close second, but with safety improvements, those numbers have dropped in the last decade.

Taken together, those mishaps account for more than half of golden eagle deaths, say researchers.

The third reason? Formerly, it was guns. A six-year shooting spree by a gun club in Texas back in the 1940s killed 5,000 golden eagles (even though it was illegal under federal law); the species still hasn't recovered in that area.

I'm happy to report that gunshots are no longer a leading cause of eagle deaths, though idiots still take aim at the birds—and are prosecuted for it. Today, accidental poisoning and traps set for fur-bearers take a bigger toll on eagles than guns.

Strong and Swift

> [23] Saul and Jonathan were lovely and pleasant in their lives, and
> in their death they were not divided: they were swifter
> than eagles, they were stronger than lions.
>
> —2 Samuel 1:23

How swift is an eagle? When a golden eagle glides with its wings partially folded—catching the air currents but not flapping—that giant body may be moving at an incredible 118 mph.

Dives are even more mind-blowing.

When an eagle spots possible prey, it folds its wings and goes into a sudden sharp dive that ornithologists call a *stoop*.

How fast is that winged doom descending on the poor jackrabbit down below?

Hang on to your hat—according to researchers, that golden eagle is plummeting at 149 to 200 mph.

Now, *that's* a sight worth waiting for.

Eating, flying, nesting—yep, eagle life is down to earth, even though the birds themselves symbolize lofty aspirations to most of us non-winged humans.

It's sheer size that makes eagles stand out. And, coupled with that sizeable bulk, the piercing, far-seeing, alert eyes.

And maybe the idea that we'd better stay on their good side, since a bird of this size, not to mention one that can kill an animal with one good squeeze of those deadly talons, is something to fear, especially in isolated areas.

Females are generally larger than males in most species of birds of prey.

In the case of our golden eagle, females weigh in at a whopping 10.8 pounds, on average; males, 7.6 pounds.

Those are averages. The biggest female ever to tip the scales was an incredible 13.6 pounds; the biggest male, just under 9.5.

That's a lotta bird, especially when it's coming straight at you at 200 mph.

A Fearsome Face

> [10] *As for the likeness of their faces, they four had the face of a man,*
> *and the face of a lion, on the right side: and they four had the face*
> *of an ox on the left side; they four also had the face of an eagle.*
>
> —Ezekiel 1:10

> [14] *And every one had four faces: the first face was the face of a*
> *cherub, and the second face was the face of a man, and the*
> *third the face of a lion, and the fourth the face of an eagle.*
>
> —Ezekiel 10:14

An eagle's face can be terrifying indeed. With eyes like lasers, fixed in an unblinking stare, that expression can only be read as "Yeah, look out, you could be next." Add the wings, and you've got a symbol of superiority that's impossible to misinterpret.

A symbol that shows up over and over in the Bible, as part of a vision. Just about every prophet in the Bible used eagle imagery to make his case.

> [4] *The first was like a lion, and had eagle's wings: I beheld till the*
> *wings thereof were plucked, and it was lifted up from the*
> *earth, and made stand upon the feet as a man, and a man's*
> *heart was given to it.*
>
> —Daniel 7:4

> [7] *And the first beast was like a lion, and the second beast like a*
> *calf, and the third beast had a face as a man, and the fourth*
> *beast was like a flying eagle.*
>
> —Revelation 4:7

In a land that hosts at least 10 species of these big, fierce birds of prey, no one needs an interpreter to get the point of these Biblical visions.

This beast does not deliver glad tidings.

EAGLE

Bald eagle (*Haliaeetus leucocephalus*)
Golden eagle (*Aquila chrysaetos*)

American range: Bald eagle, across the entire country, usually near water; golden eagle, mainly in the West but may show up anywhere.

Natural diet: Bald eagle, fish and waterfowl; golden eagle, animals and birds.

At the feeder: Not a chance. At the fishing pier? Maybe.

American species: Bald eagle, golden eagle.

Species in the Bible area: At least 10, including our own golden eagle.

A note on translation: Eagles were often combined with vultures in Bible translations. Examining the context, and the attributes to which those quotes refer, is a good way to separate the two. The Scriptures in this chapter, except for one that's noted, clearly refer to eagles. For more on translation, see Chapter 5, Birds of Prey.

Chapter 8

Falcon & Hawk

Built for Speed

[18] *Pride goeth before destruction, and a haughty spirit before a fall.*

—Proverbs 16:18

When I first discovered a website where people post their pictures of birds, I was enthralled. So much fun to share that sighting, no matter what it was.

Cedar waxwings eating berries? Great!

A nuthatch at the feeder? Yay!

Bluebird on a fencepost? Oh boy, spring is coming!

Some photos were as sharp as a professional's, but I loved the blurry, out-of-focus shots even better—they looked more like mine.

And I commented on almost every picture.

If the bird had been posted without a name, or if someone wanted help with identification, I happily filled in the blank.

Then I got my comeuppance.

"Sparrowhawk in my garden," said the title.

"That's no sparrowhawk," said I, looking at the photo.

Not wanting to sound too much like a know-it-all, I disguised my correction.

"Nice shot! Does that sharp-shinned hawk bother your feeder birds?" I commented.

Oops.

What I hadn't realized was that the website was used by people from all over the world.

Nor did I know that what I call a sparrowhawk—the American kestrel, which is a little falcon—isn't the same bird that goes by that name in Europe.

I learned my lesson.

You can't take a common name for granted. You have to look at it scientifically—from a Latin angle.

What's in a Name?

[13] *The wing of the ostrich is like the wings of the heron, and of the hawk.*

—Job 39:13, Douay-Rheims Bible

The translators of the Douay-Rheims were a little more thorough about naming birds, but they still leave us guessing, even though we understand the meaning just fine: Ostriches, herons, hawks, all have large, powerful wings. Which hawk? A big one.

But when it comes to birdwatchers and scientists, the more exact the name, the better.

Common names are the ones we use in casual conversation about birds, plants, butterflies, and other living things. And they can vary a lot from one place to another.

Take the sparrowhawk, for instance. The one that taught me a lesson in humility.

Say the name "sparrowhawk" in North America, and most bird lovers will know you're talking about the American kestrel, our most common falcon.

Say "sparrowhawk" in the Bible lands, or throughout Europe and Britain, and you're talking about a bird that looks and behaves a lot like our Cooper's hawk.

It's not a falcon at all, but an accipiter, the same group to which our sharp-shinned hawk and Cooper's hawk belong.

And it looks very much like those familiar American birds. As it should, since it's a very close relative.

The confusion around common names is why scientists use Latin binomials. They want to make sure everyone knows exactly which species is under discussion.

Why So Few Scripture Quotes?

The King James Version is the translation used as the source of the quotes in this book. And that version is mighty slim on giving hawks, falcons, and kites their due. You're much likelier to come across those words in other translations of the Bible.

Each version called upon the knowledge of its translators to get the words just right.

But whichever term is used for these birds of prey, it's most likely apropos. Because, even when there are differences between versions of the Bible, the simple truth is that these birds share enough habits and behavior to make their names interchangeable in the verses. For a deeper look at translations, and how other versions of the Bible differ from the King James Version, see Chapter 5, Birds of Prey.

"Keep It Simple, Stupid"

> [14] *and the kite, and the falcon after its kind,*
>
> —Leviticus 11:14, American Standard Version

That "Keep It Simple, Stupid" catchphrase was coined by the U.S. Navy in 1960, which expanded it to the KISS Principle, which helps ensure simplicity of design in engineering projects.

It's a good guideline for bird names, too, especially when there are so many species that detailing each by name would be a nightmare.

And the Bible writers followed it to the letter.

In a region renowned for its abundance of bird-of-prey species, just one catchall term was used for all small or slim hawks: the Hebrew word *neç.*

The blanket term is often translated as "falcon," and it does include a whole variety of falcons: 2 species of kestrels; the merlin; the peregrine falcon and 6 to 8 other species that go by the common name "falcon"; and 4 kinds of hobby, small falcons that share the "sideburns" head markings of kestrels and peregrines.

I might've missed a few, but you get the idea: There're a lot of falcons in the lands of the Bible.

But *neç* also includes some birds that aren't falcons. The Eurasian sparrowhawk, one of the most common birds of prey, falls under this term, too, as do its accipiter relatives of the area.

Who's a Hawk?

[15] *...there too the buzzards shall gather, each one with its mate.*

—Isaiah 34:15, New Revised Standard Version

In America, we separate "hawks" into five main groups:
- *Buteos:* big-bodied, bulky birds, including our abundant red-tailed hawk and other species
- *Accipiters:* Slim, swift, medium-sized birds with a typical flap-flap-glide flight pattern, including the sharp-shinned and Cooper's hawks and the bigger, somewhat stouter northern goshawk.
- *Falcons:* Sharply pointed wings and arrow-fast flight are the hallmarks of this group, which include the small-sized kestrel and merlin and the larger peregrine.
- *Harriers:* We have only one species, but it's a beauty: the northern harrier, who flies with the typical V-held wings, tilting low over marshes and fields.
- *Kites:* Separated into their own subfamily of the Accipitridae (accipiter) family, kites are slim, elegant birds that personify their name: They dance in the sky as if a skilled operator is pulling strings.

In Bible lands, "hawks" are categorized differently by common name.

- Falcons are still falcons, harriers are harriers, and kites are kites.
- Accipiters may also be called falcons. The group also includes slim-bodied birds called honey-buzzards.
- Buteos are called buzzards. (Vultures are not called buzzards.)
- Falcons, harriers, and accipiters are all grouped under the one-size-fits-all Hebrew word *neç*. That's the word used in the Bible, and those are the birds under discussion in this chapter. We'll also cover kites, which get their own Hebrew word (*dã'ah* or *dáyyah*), and thus get a shout-out in Bible translations.

You Are What You Eat

[34] *And he took and sent messes unto them from before him: but Benjamin's mess was five times so much as any of their's. And they drank, and were merry with him.*

—Genesis 43:34

Dinnertime at Joseph's house. Joseph, the favorite son of Jacob, sold into slavery by his jealous brothers many years before.

But much time had passed, and Joseph had prospered. And now he had food, while a famine gripped the land.

So he invited his father and all of his brothers to come share his food. Including Benjamin, whom Joseph hadn't seen since Benjamin was a child. Had to give him an extra-big helping, of course.

We're not sure what they were eating at that dinner of forgiveness. But we do know what sparrowhawks eat. And it's not necessarily sparrows.

The Eurasian sparrowhawk (*Accipiter nisus*) is definitely a bird eater. Every day, it snatches sparrows, finches, tits, and other small birds, as well as thrushes and starlings, right out of midair.

Our American sparrowhawk (*Falco sparverius*), on the other hand, hardly lives up to its common name.

Although it does nab small birds when the opportunity arises, it eats a lot more mice, voles, and other little rodents, with snakes, lizards, grasshoppers and other meaty insects on the side.

That's why you rarely see a sparrowhawk—the American species, that is—sitting around the bird feeder.

Its favorite foods aren't in our backyards. They're in the overgrown grassy verges of roadways and fields, which is where the bird hangs out.

Look for American kestrels along roadsides, often perched atop utility poles or clinging to the wires themselves. Watch for the bird's seesawing motions as it keeps its balance after landing, or when it's windy.

American kestrels were dubbed sparrowhawks hundreds of years ago, and many folks still know them best by that name. Seeing a kestrel snatch and pluck a small bird in flight is an unforgettable experience, and a lot more noticeable than when they prey on their usual ground-dwelling insect or rodent victims.

In the Bible region, it's the lesser kestrel (*Tinnunculus cenchris*) that fills the same niche in nature as our American species.

Give Me Wings to Fly

> ²⁶ *Doth the hawk fly by thy wisdom, and stretch her wings*
> *toward the south?*
>
> —Job 39:26

"No" is Job's only possible answer to the question God poses in this passage.

Job would've seen it for himself—the incredible migration of birds of prey, moving from Europe and Asia to Africa via the land bridge of the Bible lands. And he would've known that that massive flight had nothing to do with himself, who was only a man.

Migration is an incredible thing (and you can read more about it in Chapter 5, Birds of Prey), but so is ordinary, everyday flight.

Each kind of hawk has its own unique way of going. From the heavy, steadily flapping flight of big buteos, to the flap-flap-glide, flap-flap-glide of accipiters, to the deep dives of falcons, birds of prey are simply masters of the air.

Swiftness is the hallmark of hawks, but sometimes these wondrous creatures don't even have to make headway to make our jaws drop with wonder.

The American kestrel has a particularly neat trick. It can hover, beating its wings and remaining in the same place as the bird tries to get a better view of what's below.

A few other American hawks, including the red-tailed hawk,

the rough-legged hawk, and the northern harrier, have mastered the same technique.

Whenever you happen to spot a hawk hovering, take a few minutes, if you can, to watch what happens next.

That hovering behavior may be simply hopeful scanning. But it could be a clue that the bird may have spied possible prey below. Once the bird gets a better reading on the animal on the ground, the winged predator is likely to accelerate into a dive to try to nab it. It's a dramatic sight, and one you're likely to remember forever.

Don't be surprised, though, if the hawk comes up empty-handed. It's not easy predicting which way a rodent or other prey will run when its life is on the line.

Oh, Go Fly a Kite

*The mother flew in silence, sailed over my head just long
enough to afford me time to reload, returned, and to my great
surprise gently lifted her young, and sailing with it to another
tree, deposited it there.*

*My feelings at that moment I cannot express. I wished I had
not discovered the poor bird; for who could have witnessed,*

without emotion, so striking an example of that affection
which none but a mother can feel; so daring an act, performed
in the midst of smoke, in the presence of a dreaded and
dangerous enemy.

—John James Audubon, *Birds of America* (1840)

Shooting birds was commonplace in the 1800s, and Audubon was no exception. He "collected" birds to examine at close range and to wire into position for his paintings.

Here, he was in Louisiana, trying to get a Mississippi kite. Not much luck with the first try, a shot leveled at a youngster in the nest. But a revelation about the mother bird's behavior. Imagine that! Kites care about their offspring!

To which we might say, "Well, duh."

But no wonder Audubon wanted a specimen. Kites are cool.

Though, for some reason, I always forget about them until one flies in front of my eyes.

Kites are among our least common birds of prey, so I count myself lucky every time I see one. It's an invitation to pull over and enjoy these birds, with their buoyant flight and elegant forked tails.

One of a Kind

The osprey (*Pandion haliaetus*), a big fish-eating bird of prey that looks a lot like an eagle, gets its own family. And it's the only member of that family. Ospreys range across America, nesting near the bodies of water that supply their food. They also range across Europe and Asia, because our exact same species is shared worldwide.

Only one reference to the osprey shows up in the Bible: The prohibition against eating this bird, spelled out in both Deuteronomy and Leviticus. Birds that eat flesh aren't allowed on the table.

Like a kid's kite that loses its tether, kites have a habit of traveling erratically, far and wide. Although our five species have limited homelands, they do occasionally show up in places far beyond their normal range.

Two of our five species are total homebodies that never wander: the hook-billed kite of the extreme southern tip of Texas, and the snail kite of the Florida Everglades.

But others may show up anywhere, because their dietary needs aren't as specialized as those species. The Mississippi kite and the striking black and white swallow-tailed kite both feed on insects plucked from the air; the white-tailed kite eats rodents.

So keep your eyes open. And next time you think you've spotted a tern, take another look: That forked tail may belong to a kite.

In Bible lands, it's the red kite ("glede") and the black kite that are most commonly seen. Both have the somewhat forked tail shared by most members of this group.

The black kite looks way more like its relative, the sharp-shinned hawk, than our American kites do. And it's one of the most common birds of prey in Europe and Asia, with a population estimated at about 6 million birds.

Most elegant of the kites, in my opinion, is the African swallow-tailed kite, a pale gray bird with an extravagant tail that looks a lot like the scissor-tailed flycatcher we see in Texas and Oklahoma. Half a world separates them, of course, and several classes of birds, but at first glance, the effect is the same. And so is the reaction: "Wow!"

Oh, and as for that kite that Audubon had in his gun sights?

That tender emotion he felt about the mother bird's behavior didn't last long. Here's his less than happy ending to the story:

> *"I followed, however, and brought both to the ground at one shot, so keen is the desire of possession!"*
>
> —John James Audubon, *Birds of America* (1840)

Off the Menu

> [13] *And these are they which ye shall have in abomination among the fowls; they shall not be eaten, they are an abomination: the eagle, and the ossifrage [the lammergeyer vulture], and the ospray,*
>
> [14] *And the vulture, and the kite after his kind;*
>
> [16] *And the owl, and the night hawk, and the cuckow, and the hawk after his kind,*
>
> —Leviticus 11:13-14,16

As with all prohibitions about which birds are unfit to eat, the rules are spelled out again in Deuteronomy as well as in Leviticus. No raptors of any kind, no matter how admirable they are, can be eaten. We're limited to feasting on them with our eyes.

Falcon & Hawk
Falcons, Accipiters, Buteos, and Others

American range: Various species are found all across the country.

Natural diet: Depends on the species, but all are predators, whether it's insects, snails, or cute furry animals they set their sights on.

At the feeder: Other birds, squirrels, chipmunks.

American species: Many, including the widespread red-tailed hawk, sharp-shinned hawk, and American kestrel.

Species in the Bible area: Many.

A note on translation: Translations in various versions of the Bible vary. A lot. See also Chapter 5, Birds of Prey, for more details on Hebrew transliteration and opinions on translation regarding birds of prey.

Chapter 9

Owl

The Night Shift

[39] Therefore the wild beasts of the desert with the wild beasts of the islands shall dwell there, and the owls shall dwell therein: and it shall be no more inhabited for ever; neither shall it be dwelt in from generation to generation.

—Jeremiah 50:39

"Wild beasts," alone, is enough to instill fear in any prey, including us. No wonder many folks fear the dark.

Add eyes from the sky, and no thanks—not a place I want to wander at night.

The cover of darkness doesn't guarantee protection from predators. In fact, that's when most meat-eaters are on the prowl. And, among the feathered hunters, it's owls that work the night shift.

They can see in the dimmest of starlight. And their hearing is so acute, it's practically supersonic.

These nighttime counterparts of hawks and other birds of prey are also predators. But they don't usually get put into the same category as the daytime or *diurnal* hunters, the raptors.

They are birds of prey.

But they're not raptors.

They're owls.

Keeping Good Company

> [29] *I am a brother to dragons, and a companion to owls.*
>
> —Job 30:29

Are you having a bad day? A day when nothing goes right, and everything goes wrong?

Hey, look on the bright side—at least you're not Job.

Job fills page after page of this book of the Bible with his complaints—everything from boiling bowels to losing his wealth of sheep and cattle to being mocked by people he thought were "beneath him."

Job wasn't just having a bad day, he was having a bad day every day.

It was all part of a plan, although Job didn't know it—a plan to test his faith in God by giving him trials and tribulations.

Eventually it all works out, because Job is steadfast in his faith. But before that happy ending, he feels so forsaken, he may as well be living with owls. And dragons.

Dragons? What are they doing in here?

Welcome to the weird side of the King James Version, where dragons fume, and satyrs and unicorns make their appearance, too.

No, we haven't entered some mythical universe. We've simply stumbled upon the difficulty of translating from one language to another, especially when you have no comparable animals to match up with the words in the original writing.

The King James Version was written by Englishmen. Englishmen who'd probably never seen a jackal, and perhaps hadn't even heard of its existence. So when they came upon the Hebrew word *tannin* or its plurals, *tannim* and *tannoth,* they didn't connect it to jackals, as other translations did.

Tannin implies a howling creature, and the Bible already had a different Hebrew word for wolf, *ze'ev.*

The King James translators were familiar with wolves. Wolves were wolves. Simple. So what was this *tannin* critter?

Somehow, they made the leap to "dragon," a decision that isn't shared by nearly all other versions of the Bible.

"Jackal" is the word they were looking for, not "dragon."

But the word "owls" is right on the mark.

At first reading, this single line of Scripture seems almost kindly in tone. A companion to owls? Who wouldn't want to be friends with these intelligent birds!

Jackals, though? Not so much. Maybe we'd better read more.

And that's when we find out that Job is bemoaning his problems, and feeling isolated not only from other people, but from God.

"I'm like a jackal," he moans. And nobody likes jackals.

"I'm only fit to keep company with owls." Hate to break it to him, but even those birds probably wouldn't want his company.

Parallel Owls

Some of our owls are exactly the same as those of Bible lands—they're worldwide species, not only North American. Others have close counterparts there, sharing similar habits and homes.

North American owls	Counterpart in Bible lands
Great horned owl (*Bubo virginianus*)	Eurasian eagle owl (*Bubo bubo*)
Screech owls (*Megascops* species)	Scops owls (*Otus* species)
Burrowing owl (*Athene cunicularia*)	Burrowing owl or little owl (*Athene noctua*)
Long-eared owl (*Asio otus*)	*Same species*
Short-eared owl (*Asio flammeus*)	*Same species*
Barn owl (*Tyto alba*)	*Same species*

Single Room, Please

15 There shall the great owl make her nest, and lay, and hatch, and gather under her shadow: there shall the vultures also be gathered, every one with her mate.

—Isaiah 34:15

Owls are devoted family birds, and companionable couples—at breeding time. Pairs mate for life, and in the case of our great horned owl, that can be 20 years or more.

Most owls hunt actively just after sunset, for a period that lasts two to three hours, and again in the hours before dawn. Then they find a roosting place to digest, or to sleep away the daytime.

During the breeding season, which starts in late winter, owls roost near or on the nest.

Their bedroom is any perch where they're out of sight of daytime birds: a conifer or other dense tree, a tangle of shrubbery, a rock ledge, or a barn loft or other owl-accessible part of a human structure.

And that sleeping place has to be very near the nest, when it's holding eggs or fuzzy-headed babies. The dedicated couple roost close together, keeping an eye on the family home.

Outside of nesting season? Well, let's just say the couple usually doesn't kiss goodnight.

Once those fledglings fly the coop, the male bird is outta there. Instead of cuddling up together, each parent sleeps wherever that night's foraging happens to end.

The pair continues to share the same territory, but they don't hang out together until the next breeding cycle rolls around. Although the male continues helping out by feeding the youngsters until they learn the tricks of the trade, it's separate bedrooms at night for the mister and missus.

When they're not busy with the kids, owls prefer to go it alone.

Descending Doom

> [14] *The wild beasts of the desert shall also meet with the wild beasts of the island, and the satyr shall cry to his fellow; the screech owl also shall rest there, and find for herself a place of rest.*
>
> —Isaiah 34:14

Resting screech owls, hm? I had them once, a family who'd nested in a dead snag of a big old sugar maple outside my door, and still used the tree as a roost at night.

And I never even thought twice the summer evening I released 50-some big, gorgeous cecropia moths into the night.

I'd raised those moths from eggs that someone gave me. Nurtured them through weeks of steady eating. Snitched black walnut leaves for them from neighbors' yards, when I ran out.

And now, after hatching from their big brown silken cocoons, they were ready to fly.

Oops.

As soon as the first moth wings fluttered towards the street light, the screech owls resting nearby sprang into action. *Snap! Snap! Snap!* went their beaks, as my moths met a fate I'd never imagined.

At least they didn't suffer. In fact, they probably never even knew what hit 'em.

Sudden Death

It must be the very worst way to wake up, when you're a duck sleeping on the water: A sudden death grip from above, squeezing so tight you don't even have time to get out a feeble squawk before you're done for.

That's the hunting technique of owls. Most prey on rodents and small birds, but the great horned owl takes ducks, coots, and other waterfowl, plus any furred creatures it can get into its grip.

One night, when I stepped outside after midnight, an all-white cat walking across the black-topped parking lot across the street caught my attention. How could it not? The white animal stuck out like a sore thumb, even at night.

Unfortunately for the cat, I wasn't the only one who noticed it.

A great horned owl swooped in from behind, struck the cat with its feet, and lifted off without missing a beat of its great silent wings. The cat dangled limply from the owl's talons, already dead, as the bird gained altitude and flapped away.

The whole episode, which took just seconds, was weirdly and utterly silent. The cat's feet, crossing the paving, made no sound. The owl's feathers, swooping in for the kill, made no sound. And neither participant said a word during the fatal-for-one encounter.

Stunning.

That Stinks!

"Must be a skunk around," I thought, as that unmistakable bouquet wafted to my nose on a walk in the woods.

The smell got stronger, and my wariness increased. Then I saw the source. Not a skunk, but a great horned owl, which was lying dead in the path.

These big owls have a real fondness for skunk meat, and preying upon the black-and-white animals leaves a signature scent.

Judging from the strength of the stink, this owl had tangled with a skunk very recently. When I stretched out a wing to admire the soft feathers, I saw that the owl had been shot while flying—the bullet hole went into his side, just below the wing. An illegal act, as well as a reprehensible one.

Glad the poor guy got to enjoy his favorite food for his last meal.

Sing We Now

⁸ *Therefore I will wail and howl, I will go stripped and naked: I
will make a wailing like the dragons, and mourning as the owls.*

—Micah 1:8

Wailing in a soprano like jackals ("dragons"), hooting in bass like owls—what a recital that must've been.

Sonorous notes are the calling card of the great horned owl, but they're not the only sound that owls make. Some add a dash of whinnies, syncopated hoots, rhythmic handsaw strokes, maniacal laughs, plus strange hisses and the percussion of snapping bills. It's a full symphony of weirdness.

Owls may call any time of year, but it's in winter that they really go into full gear. Breeding season is starting, and every owl around is advertising for a partner and warning others of its species to stay away.

These fascinating birds cover the country. Forests, deserts, fields, grassland, deserts—there's an owl for every type of habitat, with many of them adapting to all sorts of homegrounds.

Because their comings and goings are hidden by the dark, we often don't even know that they may be living right near our own houses, or in the surrounding countryside.

Listening for an owl at night is a great way to tell who's at home in your neighborhood.

And talking back is just plain fun.

When you hear an owl, cup your hands around your mouth, face the direction the sound is coming from, and imitate the call. Even a crude imitation is enough to draw a curious owl closer.

One summer night, I learned to my chagrin that even my loud laugh may sound like a potential partner to a barred owl. As I hooted and cackled with my friends on the patio, the big bird silently winged in to the tree above me and let loose a stream of "laughter" of its own. Which only made me laugh all the louder.

Owls Underground

Owls nest in all sorts of places—in dead snags or holes in trees, in barns, in the abandoned nests of red-tailed hawks, in saguaro cactuses. But the strangest nesting place of all is claimed by the burrowing owls of American and worldwide deserts and grasslands.

[6] I am like a pelican of the wilderness: I am like an owl of the desert.
                                                              —Psalms 102:6

Punishing heat and glaring sun are the rule in these mostly treeless expanses, and a home below ground keeps the birds cool. A burrow also helps protect the owls from the many raptors that cruise the skies. And it provides easy access to prey, which, in American species, is largely insects.

Although burrowing owls often live among prairie dogs or other ground squirrels, these rodents aren't usually on the menu. Instead, the animals and owls help each other, by keeping a double lookout for approaching danger.

The Lure of Water

> [20] *The beasts of the field shall honour me, the dragons and the*
> *owls: because I give waters in the wilderness, and rivers in the*
> *desert, to give drink to my people, my chosen.*
>
> —Isaiah 43:20

Owls aren't big on bathing, but they very much appreciate the living feast that is drawn to a natural source of water.

Songbirds are likely to be nesting there. Rabbits and rodents will be plentiful because of the vegetation. Ducks and other waterfowl may settle on the river or its banks.

All in all, a source of water means a smorgasbord for a hunting owl. Thanks for the water!

Home Alone

> [21] *But wild beasts of the desert shall lie there; and their houses*
> *shall be full of doleful creatures; and owls shall dwell there,*
> *and satyrs shall dance there.*
>
> —Isaiah 13:21

> [11] *But the cormorant and the bittern shall possess it; the owl also*
> *and the raven shall dwell in it: and he shall stretch out upon it*
> *the line of confusion, and the stones of emptiness.*
>
> —Isaiah 34:11

These sections of Isaiah always make me get goosebumps.

I'm not a big fan of horror movies—in fact, I've never seen one—but the voice of an owl can be downright creepy.

Weird sounds, and we can't see who's making them?

Yep, there go the goosebumps.

Not to mention, the scene that's painted in these verses reminds me of the unearthly, spine-chilling landscapes of Salvador Dali or El Greco.

So, yeah. After the destruction about to be wrought by God, the kingdom of Judah was not going to be a happy place.

Not for people, anyway. Half-people, maybe. Like that satyr mentioned in Isaiah 34:14. Who, according to other translations and to Biblical scholars, should have been a "hairy goat."

But owls—hey, they're going to feel right at home, there in the deserted land.

> ^{15} *There shall the great owl make her nest, and lay, and hatch, and gather under her shadow: there shall the vultures also be gathered, every one with her mate.*
>
> —Isaiah 34:15

While some species of owls nest near human habitation, or frequent our backyards to pick off rodents and sleeping birds, these predators still prefer privacy. The more they escape our notice, the happier they are.

Some owls, including the little screech owl, quickly adopt a knothole in a tree or a nest box in our backyards.

Barn owls move into haylofts, sheds, and factories.

But even these birds rely on the cover of darkness to hide their activities from our eyes.

Other owls, such as the great horned, the long-eared, and the short-eared, stick to areas that are away from anything more than the very occasional human presence.

And some are true hermits, living deep in forests or in burrows in the desert.

> ^{13} *And thorns shall come up in her palaces, nettles and brambles in the fortresses thereof: and it shall be an habitation of dragons, and a court for owls.*
>
> —Isaiah 34:13

Around the nest, all owls are extremely secretive. If a person is nearby, they won't bring food to their babies.

Hiding in plain sight is par for the course for owls.

When they're resting during the daytime, owls stay on the down low, too. Their mottled feathers blend in perfectly with tree bark, and they often perch right up against the trunk, where their silhouette won't stand out.

> [39] *Therefore the wild beasts of the desert with the wild beasts of the islands shall dwell there, and the owls shall dwell therein: and it shall be no more inhabited for ever; neither shall it be dwelt in from generation to generation.*
>
> —Jeremiah 50:39

So, sure, the new real estate God was creating would suit the owls just fine. The rubble of Jerusalem and Babylon? Perfect place to tuck a nest into the tumbled masonry.

Owl Omelette?

> [15] *And the owl, and the night hawk, and the cuckow, and the hawk after his kind,*
>
> [16] *The little owl, and the great owl, and the swan,*
>
> —Deuteronomy 14:15-16

Echoed by Leviticus, the rules in Deuteronomy are clear: No owl, no little owl, no great owl.

Even though we don't know exactly which species are included, we get the idea: No owls of any size.

No owls.

OWL

Great Horned, Barn, and Other Owls

American range: Great horned owl, barn owl, and screech owl, all across America; burrowing owl and other species have more limited or seasonal ranges.

At the feeder: Animals that visit your feeder at night for spilled birdseed, including mice and other rodents, flying squirrels, opossums, and skunks, might put your backyard on a neighborhood owl's nightly route.

American species: 19 species, from the tiny elf owl to the huge snowy owl.

Species in the Bible area: More than a dozen species, including our barn owl.

A note on translation: The Hebrew transliteration for owl is *wa·'eṯ*; adjectives applied to it create "the little owl," "the great owl," and other variations.

Chapter 10

Quail & Partridge
Bon Appetit

²⁰ *Now therefore, let not my blood fall to the earth before the face of the Lord: for the king of Israel is come out to seek a flea, as when one doth hunt a partridge in the mountains.*

—1 Samuel 26:20

It was my first visit to Rocky Mountain National Park, and it was supposed to be a pleasant detour on the way home from a long road trip with husband Matt.

Below the park, it'd been a fine autumn day, with aspens in full golden glory. So warm, I was perfectly comfy in a long-sleeved tee shirt. With the sleeves pushed up to the elbows.

But as soon as we entered the park and started to climb, all that changed in a hurry.

Up here, it was winter. Snow, fog, sleet, a brutally cold wind.

At the summit of the drive—the innocently named Trail Ridge Road—the clouds hung so low, it looked like a billowy bed of cotton when I peered out my passenger-seat window.

Which was a good thing. Because, had I known what precipitous heights we were traveling on that steep, narrow, winding road, I would've bitten my fingernails down to the knuckles.

No getting out and exploring, as we'd thought we might do. The goal quickly became "get through these 12,000-foot mountains alive."

At the very highest point, where trees had long since petered out to tundra, a bird suddenly appeared beside the road.

A bird neither of us had ever seen before.

And we see a lot of birds.

This one was a white-tailed ptarmigan, its umber feathers splotched with white like a pinto pony. It was changing to winter plumage to match the snow.

Then, right before our eyes, the big bird vanished into the rapidly whitening landscape of ground-hugging alpine plants.

"Where'd it go?"

"You see it?"

"No. You?"

Forgetting about the fact that we needed to get down from the mountain while conditions were still drivable, we stopped the car and peered into the tundra with binoculars. Even with our vision magnified seven times, the ptarmigan was invisible.

"Seeking a flea," indeed.

And a Partridge in a Pear Tree

> *...Four calling birds, three French hens, two turtledoves, and a partridge in a pear tree.*

> —Traditional English carol

Ptarmigans are as close as we get to partridges in North America.

The only partridges in America, the chukar and the gray partridge (a British species, of "Twelve Days of Christmas" renown), were brought in by hunting clubs, and usually need regular replenishing.

Some populations have managed to carve out a small niche for themselves and settled in to our American landscape.

In the high desert of eastern Oregon, some areas of the Rockies, and a few other areas, you may spot chukars scuttling about.

But in the lands of the Bible, as well as elsewhere in Europe, Asia, and Africa, partridges are common.

Fifty-species common.

That's a huge number of different kinds of birds, each species adapted to its own surroundings.

As for that partridge in a pear tree, it wasn't at a nest, even though Christmas cards often show that scene.

These birds nest on the ground, no matter which of the 50-some partridge species they belong to.

Homes on High

Like our North American ptarmigans of the high Rockies and other peaks, partridges range over the mountains of the Old World.

From the Alps to the Himalayas to the Apennines to the Al-Nusayriyah of Syria to any other Old World mountain range you care to name, partridges are hunkered down in high places.

Some of the more than 50 species live at lower elevations. But each has its preferred niche, whether that's farmland on the plains or the starkest tundra atop a high peak.

Partridges don't migrate. They live year-round in a given area, which sure helps keep them sorted out.

In the lands of the Bible, it's easy to pinpoint the partridges. Only three species scurry about:

- The *chukar*—yep, same bird that's now at home in some small areas in the U.S., where it was brought in for hunting—lives both in the highlands and on the plains.
- The *sand partridge* settles in sandy, dry, hilly areas.
- The *black francolin,* which looks like a short-tailed pheasant, stays in cultivated lands near water, with thick vegetation where it can stay out of sight.

Better than a Baker's Dozen

> [11] *As the partridge sitteth on eggs, and hatcheth them not; so he that getteth riches, and not by right, shall leave them in the midst of his days, and at his end shall be a fool.*
>
> —Jeremiah 17:11

A partridge nest holds from half a dozen to as many as 20 eggs.

And no way would the mother hen leave that treasure alone for very long, although she may make a quick trip away from the nest to feed herself.

She incubates the eggs with tender care, for more than three full weeks.

And should the eggs fail to hatch, perhaps because of bad weather, perhaps because of destruction by a predator, the hen soon lays a new batch.

No fool, she.

You're Chicken!

> *Galliformes*, from the Latin *gallina*, "hen," and *gallus*, "cock"
>
> —*Merriam-Webster Dictionary*

Well, no, of course you're not chicken. But partridges and ptarmigans are.

In a family sense, that is.

These birds are members of the order Galliformes, or *gallinaceous birds*—birds that are related to chickens.

Like chickens, all members of the gallinaceous gang have heavy, plump bodies.

Mmm, good eating!

In the Old World—that'd be the continents of Europe, Asia, Africa, and Australia—gallinaceous birds abound.

Yep. Lots and lots of fowls.

These are the homelands of pheasants, grouse, peacocks, turkeys, chickens, guinea fowl, and more kinds of partridges and quail than you can shake a stick at.

Counting Our Chickens

In the New World—that's us, plus Central and South America—partridges are paltry.

Except for a few species of quail and grouse, so are the other gallinaceous birds.

Nearly all of the species that strut or scuttle about this continent have been imported as domestic fowl, or as gamebirds by hunting clubs.

Sorry, chickens aren't American. The ancestors of our domesticated drumsticks originated in India.

Our wild turkeys are all-American—but even they had to be reintroduced to most areas, after they died out because of hunting and habitat destruction. They've bounced back, though, and in a big way.

Those gorgeous pheasants stalking proudly through the cornfields? Not ours, either; their ancestral home is in China. We brought them here for hunting.

Then again, we do have the Old World beat in one regard. We've got ptarmigans.

Oh, wait, no, we don't, not exclusively—our rock ptarmigan (*Lagopus muta*) also roams the high places of northern Europe, Russia, and Japan.

And we have to share the willow ptarmigan (*Lagopus lagopus*) of Alaska and Canada, too: It's native right across the whole top swath of Europe.

Only the white-tailed ptarmigan (*Lagopus leucera*)—the bird Matt and I saw for a brief instant on that snowy autumn day in the highest Rockies—is ours alone.

Yet, even its name comes from the Old World: from the Scottish Gaelic *tàrmachan*.

Fine.

At least we've got some very nice quail.

Good Eats

[40] *The people asked, and he brought quails, and satisfied them with the bread of heaven.*

—Psalms 105:40

Now that's some good eatin'!

Although, I'm sorry to say, I've never tasted quail, it apparently is tender and delicious.

Tastes like…. Yep. You guessed it. Chicken.

Dark meat chicken.

Quail have been high on the menu of wild foods for thousands of years.

Unlike partridges and ptarmigans, which are solitary by nature, not to mention as hard to find as a flea in the mountains, cute little quail run around in flocks, or coveys. One cast of a net, and you have a week's worth of meals.

Not for me, though. Though I happily eat chicken without a qualm, I'd rather keep my quail appreciation reserved for the living birds.

Quail are cute.

Sorry, but there's no other word for that little fat ball of feathers, especially when a covey scurries past single-file, each one running as fast as its short little legs will go.

Add a goofy bobbing topknot, as in our California and Gambel's species, and you can't help but say "Aww."

Cute, Times Six

We have six species of quail living in various parts of the country, five of them in the West and the northern bobwhite in the eastern half of the country.

The Montezuma quail and the bobwhite are the littlest guys in

the group, around 9 to 10 inches long, but our other American species aren't much bigger.

All have short, stubby wings, and only fly when they absolutely have to. Quail are great at running, and that's how they get
about most of the time, usually choosing a route that keeps them at
least partly hidden in grass or brush.

But when push comes to shove, and it's time to take to the air,
quail become feathered rockets. They zoom up from the ground,
scattering in all directions.

That habit makes them a favorite challenge for hunters. Hard
to predict which way they'll fly, let alone center a gunsight on the
fast little birds.

After alighting a safe distance from whatever danger caused
such alarm, the covey calls to each other in soft little voices as the
birds scurry towards each other—on the ground, under cover—to
knit the flock back together.

Yay! The gang's all here again. Time to get back to the business
of eating bugs and pecking at plants.

Dart and Dash

When they're crossing open space, quail look like they're playing a
scene from an old Western movie.

They dart from rock to rock (or any other cover, including any
car that happens to be parked along their route), pause and peer
out, then make another dash.

That's self-protection at work. Hawks, foxes, and a whole slew
of other predators love quail as much as the Israelites in the Bible
and today's fine-food aficionados. Did we mention they taste like
chicken?

Traveling Quail

> [12] *I have heard the murmurings of the children of Israel: speak unto them, saying, At even ye shall eat flesh, and in the morning ye shall be filled with bread; and ye shall know that I am the Lord your God.*
>
> [13] *And it came to pass, that at even the quails came up, and covered the camp: and in the morning the dew lay round about the host.*
>
> —Exodus 16:12-13

This is just one part of a great Bible story, the story of the Exodus of the Israelites. And it's a good one—a feast of plenty, arriving just when the travelers were at the end of their rope.

It was hard times for the Israelites on the journey. Food was scarce—make that, practically nonexistent—as they made their way across the desert.

Then came a rain of quail from the sky, a feast for all.

Saved!

What kind of quail? Easy—there's only one species in the Bible lands. It's called, quite appropriately, the common quail (*Coturnix coturnix*), a rotund little bird that looks a lot like our bobwhite.

And it's common, indeed. Way, way common. Hundreds of millions of the birds range across Europe and Asia.

Normally, these quail live in groups, or coveys, in farmlands and grasslands. There may be a dozen or more birds in the group.

The covey sticks together, scooting about to peck at seeds and bugs or tender buds.

Preferring to trust their feet and camouflage coloring, rather than take to the wing to escape danger, they're reluctant to fly.

Except when it's migration time.

And here's the big difference between the common quail of Eurasia and our bobwhite and other American species: This bird is a migrant.

The only migrant quail.

And a migrant who flies at night.

A Fly-by-Night Trip

> [31] And there went forth a wind from the Lord, and brought quails from the sea, and let them fall by the camp, as it were a day's journey on this side, and as it were a day's journey on the other side, round about the camp, and as it were two cubits high upon the face of the earth.
>
> —Numbers 11:31

Imagine the wide, wide expanse of Europe and Asia, from the islands of Britain to Siberia.

Imagine all of the quail in that wide expanse.

Imagine them all moving to Africa for the winter. (Except for some that go to India.)

Where do they cross from one continent to the other?

Most, right in the lands of the Bible. Skirting the edge—and often flying over the water—of the Mediterranean.

Millions upon millions of the small, plump birds. Pushing their stubby wings to the limit as they make the incredible journey in wave after wave.

It's dark. The birds are navigating by the stars, and also by keeping track of the magnetism of the Earth.

Now, up comes a storm. The night sky is blotted out by clouds. And worse yet, winds push fiercely against those feathered bodies.

Can't... keep... on... the... route....

And the immense flock, thousands upon thousands strong, yields to the gale, and is blown through the sky.

When the wind abates, their exhausted little bodies tumble down to earth.

Where are we?

Oh. At the camp of the Israelites.

Uh-oh.

Birds blown off course during migration typically rest up for a few days before they get back on their way.

These quail, though, had no chance for a nice, long, leisurely recuperation.

They had a dinner date. Or maybe it was breakfast.

A Multitude of Quail

> [32] *And the people stood up all that day, and all that night, and all the next day, and they gathered the quails: he that gathered least gathered ten homers: and they spread them all abroad for themselves round about the camp.*
>
> —Numbers 11:32

"C'mon everybody, stop rubbing your eyes in disbelief! Grab those quail, and let's eat!"

Quail are small birds. A live northern bobwhite weighs in at about 5 to 6 ounces, and once you remove the feathers, feet, and other extraneous parts, you're left with just a few good bites of meat.

Most cooks figure on two birds to serve one person.

God, though, had other ideas.

When God supplied quail, it was a two-day all-you-can-eat feast, and plenty to set aside for later.

Two cubits deep, as we read in Numbers 11:31. Which means, roughly, a 3-feet-deep layer of quail.

Yet even that abundance barely made a dent in the population of the common quail.

A 2013 estimate by the International Union for Conservation of Nature (IUCN), which monitors population trends, notes, "a very preliminary estimate of the global population size is 35,000,000-300,000,000 individuals."

That's a lot of quail. And, even if you're not there to pick them up when they fall from the skies, still much easier to catch for dinner than "seeking a flea" of a partridge in the mountains.

QUAIL, PARTRIDGES, PTARMIGANS
Various species

American range: Ptarmigans, only in the Far North and in some high mountains; quail, widely distributed; partridges introduced for hunting purposes, only in limited areas.

Natural diet: Seeds, insects, leaves, flowers, buds.

At the feeder: Ptarmigans don't visit feeders, but quail come for millet, milo, cracked corn. Quail love water, and will eagerly drink from a low basin or pedestal-type birdbath.

American species: Northern bobwhite, California quail, Gambel's quail, scaled quail, mountain quail; white-tailed ptarmigan, willow ptarmigan, rock ptarmigan; nonnative chukar and gray partridge.

Species in the Bible area: Common quail; chukar, sand partridge, black francolin.

A note on translation: The Hebrew transliteration *is śə·lāw*, quail; *qō·rê,* partridge.

Chapter 11

Dove

The Voice of the Turtle

*12 The flowers appear on the earth; the time of the singing of
birds is come, and the voice of the turtle is heard in our land;*

—Song of Solomon 2:12

Voice of the turtle? What? Turtles don't speak.

No. But turtledoves do.

And that's what King Solomon was referring to.

"Turtle" is simply shorthand for turtledove.

And the name "turtledove" has nothing to do with any resemblance to turtles.

Turtur is the Latin name for a genus that includes several species of doves.

It's not a Latin word at all, though—it has no meaning in that language or in any other. It's onomatopoeia: a phonetic representation of the actual voice of the dove.

And it's very similar to the Hebrew word for turtledove: *tôr,* another syllable that echoes the voice of a dove.

Say the name *Turtur* with a long U in each syllable, and you'll see what I mean.

Not *ter-ter*—which is where that corruption to "turtle" comes from—but *tuuur, tuuur.*

Hey, I hear a dove! Well, sort of. Today, most of us would just say, doves "coo."

The Bible isn't the only place where turtledoves became turtles. Shakespeare used the same terminology in his allegorical poem, "The Phoenix and the Turtle," about the love affair between two unlikely birds:

> *So between them love did shine,*
> *That the turtle saw his right*
> *Flaming in the phoenix' sight:*
> *Either was the other's mine.*

Miracle Muscles

How do doves make that cooing or *tuuuring* sound? With special muscles that work at high speed to push air that creates vibrations.

Research on ringneck doves revealed specialized muscles that vibrate at warp speed to send air up from the bird's lungs.

These muscles contract fast and furious. How fast? About ten times more rapidly than the contractions of the muscles we use for running at top speed.

As the rapid bursts of air pass over the bird's larynx, it creates that trademark quavering *cooo.*

So far, the dove is the only bird that's known to have this kind of muscle.

Rattlesnakes have them, too, and use them to "shake, rattle, and roll" their warning tail.

Feathered "Turtles"

> [19] *And out of the ground the Lord God formed every beast of the field, and every fowl of the air; and brought them unto Adam to see what he would call them: and whatsoever Adam called every living creature, that was the name thereof.*
>
> —Genesis 2:19

Whether we call them "turtles," as perhaps Adam dubbed them, or add the word "dove" to their name, these birds are abundant in Bible lands.

The most common is the turtledove, also known as the Eurasian or European turtledove. It once bore the formal scientific name of *Turtur vulgaris*—which means "the common *tuuuuur-tuuuuurer*."

Those who classify living things sometimes change those classifications, and thus their official Latin names. Nowadays, this turtledove is scientifically known as *Streptopelia turtur*. Glad to see it still has *turtur* in there.

In America, the mourning dove is our most common and abundant species. Which is a nice way of saying, there are zillions.

Talk to countryfolk, and you may hear this bird called a turtledove. The name endures, perhaps because of Biblical references.

We have another ten or so species of doves and pigeons, but except for the widespread rock pigeon, the others have a much smaller range or are much less abundant than our friend the mourning dove.

Hundreds of species of doves and pigeons roam the world. In the Bible lands, at least a dozen species are common, with others passing through on migration between Africa and Europe or Asia.

Still, it's the turtledove that rules the roost there, just as the mourning dove does in our own country.

Not only the plain old turtledove: the Oriental turtledove (also known as the Eastern turtledove or the rufous turtledove) and the palm turtledove are also common birds in the Mideast, along with a variety of other doves.

And let's not forget pigeons, a bigger version of doves. While North America is limited to the rock pigeon, the lands of the Bible are home to three species: the rock pigeon (yep, same bird we have), the wood pigeon, and the stock pigeon.

With all those birds in residence, cooing would be pretty much a constant background noise.

Formal Introduction

If you're new to scientific names, think of them as *your* name, but with last name first.

"Smith John" instead of John Smith, for instance.

Just like "Smith John," Latin names are two-parted, or *binomial*.

First comes the name of the genus—the group called Smith.

Then, to narrow it down further, comes "John." In the case of scientific names, that's called the *specific epithet*. It pinpoints the particular species ("specific") within that genus.

Why Latin? Because that's the common language of scientific names around the world.

The Voice of Love

^{14} Like a crane or a swallow, so did I chatter: I did mourn as a dove: mine eyes fail with looking upward. O Lord, I am oppressed; undertake for me.

—Isaiah 38:14

Everyone knows what a dove looks like. Even if we can't name the particular kind of dove (or pigeon), we recognize these distinctive small-headed, big-bodied birds at a glance.

And most of us know what they sound like, too—they coo, making a sound just like that word.

No harsh squawks, no shrill cries, no long sweet songs that go all over the scale.

Nope, with doves, it's mainly a one-note performance, *coo, coo, coo*. Or *ooo, ooo, ooo*, because often that hard C we put in front is lacking in real life.

Many species have more of a purring note ("*tuuuur tuuuur*"), but the gentle, repeated song is still instantly recognizable as the voice of a dove.

Repeated a zillion times, of course. Because when that's all you've got, well, it's what you're gonna use to attract a mate, to sing for joy, to warn away intruders, or to serve any other purpose.

Each dove species has its own variations on the theme. Our American mourning doves do a slightly syncopated *coo-ahh-coo-coo-coo* at times. But, generally speaking, it's all cooing, all the time.

Why So Sad?

Many doves hold forth in a minor key, and in low-pitched tones. Combine that with the plaintive effect of simple, long-held notes, add a very slight quaver, and it sure sounds sad.

> *[11] We roar all like bears, and mourn sore like doves: we look for judgment, but there is none; for salvation, but it is far off from us.*
>
> —Isaiah 59:11

Doves may sound mournful, but that's our own ear putting a spin on their voices. Doves aren't sad at all when they're singing. They're proud, hopeful, even defiant.

Unlike most other bird species, doves don't have an array of decidedly different calls to indicate what's behind the vocalizing.

When an American robin or a batch of house sparrows go into their harsh, scolding calls, we know right away that something is causing them alarm.

But a dove's alarm call sounds only slightly different than its usual cooing. To the casual ear, it's hard to tell the difference.

Even when a snake slithers up to its nest, for instance, all a dove can say is "*Coo.*" Maybe a little more frantically, and with a slightly different inflection, but all in all, not so different from its usual note.

Still, it's hard for us to set aside our own feelings at what, to our ears, is the decidedly mournful call of a dove, especially when a male dove is singing its long, drawn-out love song.

It makes for a fine analogy to indicate utter despair in the Bible. But it's not sad, to the ear of a dove.

Cleaving Only unto Each Other

> *[2] I sleep, but my heart waketh; it is the voice of my beloved that knocketh, saying, Open to me, my sister, my love, my dove, my undefiled: for my head is filled with dew, and my locks with the drops of the night.*
>
> —Song of Solomon 5:2

Feeling lovey-dovey? Sentimentality is natural when you're in love, and doves are a fine symbol of romance. They're devoted partners. Many species stay with the same mate until death doth them part.

That's not unusual in the world of birds.

Many other bird species do the same thing. They raise a family with the same partner, year after year.

For most birds, though, it's not exactly a "forsaking all others" kind of arrangement.

Although the pair commits to building a nest and caring for a family, there's still room for extracurricular liaisons in most species of birds.

Both the male and female of the couple may engage in such behavior, even when their mate tries to discourage it by maintaining an alert vigil and driving away competitors.

Protecting the Investment

There's a lot at stake in the pairing of a couple of birds.

Raising a nestful of babies is hard work, usually requiring both parents to spend all day, every day, gathering food to stuff down those hungry gullets every few minutes.

If the eggs in the nest are from various sires, the male of the couple is rightfully reluctant to invest so much energy raising a family that doesn't carry his own genes.

In some species, too many flings can lead to a "divorce," as even ornithologists call it. Male mountain bluebirds, for example, have been known to desert a spouse, should she show herself to be too much of a flirt.

What *is* unusual about doves—and one of the big reasons they signify enduring love—is that most species don't even think about expanding their horizons, so to speak.

Theirs is not an open marriage.

The bond is between the pair, and the pair alone.

Maybe that's because they're too busy to think about anything else besides feeding the family.

Slapdash Nests

We're not talking fine architecture here. With doves, it's slap a bunch of sticks together, and call it good. Stand underneath the nest of a mourning dove, our most common American species, and you'll see sky right through the flimsy platform.

Most dove species lay only two eggs in that slapped-together nest. Still, when you calculate the number of nestings each year, it's no wonder doves are among the most abundant birds in the world.

One Nest After Another

> [7] *Yea, the stork in the heaven knoweth her appointed times; and*
> *the turtle and the crane and the swallow observe the time of*
> *their coming; but my people know not the judgment of the Lord.*
>
> —Jeremiah 8:7

Just as the prophet Jeremiah and King Solomon said, the dove— okay, turtle—is a harbinger of spring.

Some dove species migrate; others don't. Those that do travel are early arrivals in the waves of birds that pass through.

A big majority of bird species raise only one batch of babies a year. Mostly, it's a matter of having enough time. Migrant birds need to fit in the entire family process in the few short months between their arrival in spring and their departure in fall.

Weather is a limiting factor, too.

Early nesters, including bluebirds and tree swallows, often get into trouble when a late spring cold snap causes insects—their main food—to disappear.

Even birds that live with us year-round need to have the building supplies, the bugs, the warmth to keep their nestlings in fine fettle. So, it's once-and-done for many birds.

Song sparrows, eastern bluebirds, cardinals, and some other species may squeeze in a second nesting, and even a third, since they don't have to leave, come fall.

Other resident birds, such as chickadees, raise only one brood, even though they usually get an early start on the season.

But doves? Um, can you say "rabbits"? These birds breed as fast and furious as a couple of bunnies.

Ten nestings a year—even one every month—is typical for mourning doves in mild-winter areas.

The parents start work on the next nest, sometimes even laying eggs, before the previous brood has flown the coop.

Think Spring

Doves are among the earliest birds to begin nesting. And cooing begins even earlier, as males advertise for a mate.

Doves vocalize most when they're pairing up, beginning in late winter. In many regions, that "appointed time" mentioned in Jeremiah 8:7 is right around Valentine's Day.

Hey, Get a Room

> [9] *My dove, my undefiled is but one; she is the only one of her*
> *mother, she is the choice one of her that bare her. The*
> *daughters saw her, and blessed her; yea, the queens and the*
> *concubines, and they praised her.*
>
> —Song of Solomon 6:9

Doves have been a popular motif on Valentines, wedding wishes, and anniversary cards for hundreds of years.

Browse through a box of old postcards, and you're bound to soon come across a pair of doves. Perched side by side, flying together, or otherwise keeping close company. And usually surrounded with flowers and ribbons, just to heighten the romance.

Likening a sweetheart to a dove is a compliment. But that "undefiled" state isn't going to last long.

Unlike most birds, doves aren't very shy—either around us, or around each other.

Their public displays of affection are right out in the open for us to see, in our own backyards, on utility wires, anywhere a pair of doves happens to perch.

Doves do look like a romantic couple when they're engaged in courtship behavior. For one thing, they kiss.

Ornithologists call this *billing and cooing,* and that's a pretty much literal description of what's going on. Doves say *coooo*—a lot. Vocalizing is part of their courtship.

As for that "billing," it sure looks a lot like human kissing and petting.

The male inserts his bill into the female's as they waggle their heads back and forth. Warning: not so romantic detail coming—sometimes the male regurgitates a bit of "crop milk" as a treat.

He also fondles her, winnowing gently through her feathers with his bill. The head and neck get the most attention in this affectionate gesture, which biologists call *allopreening.*

Got Milk?

Even in cold areas, doves and pigeons can successfully raise a family before winter completely loses its grip. Other birds have to wait for soft-bodied insects to satisfy their nestlings' seemingly endless appetites. But doves have a secret weapon: "crop milk," also called "pigeon milk."

As long as the parent doves or pigeons can feed themselves—and they generally can, because the seeds, grain, and birdfeeder offerings they depend on are available year-round—both male and female are able to produce super-nutritious crop milk for nestlings.

It's not regurgitated partly-digested food, as you might think. It's food produced by lactation, just as the breasts of mammals produce milk for their young.

The lumpy whitish yellow fluid consists of cells that are sloughed off the parent's own crop. It may sound gross, but this is a super-nutritious food, rich in fat, protein, antioxidants, and other good stuff. And doves aren't the only birds that produce it—penguins and flamingos do, too.

Both male and female doves and pigeons (and flamingos) produce crop milk; in penguins, it's only the male who lactates.

Crop milk is all the nestlings eat for their first several days of their life. Then, like human infants graduating to jars of baby food, the young doves or pigeons get switched to regurgitated grain and fruit until they leave home.

The Dark Side of Dove Romance

Other parts of the "romance" between doves don't look quite so pretty to us in real life. Consider the behavior that ornithologists call *driving*. If you feed doves in your yard, you've no doubt seen it yourself, especially in early spring, when the birds are forming pair bonds for nesting.

Like a creepy guy at the corner bar, male doves can be way too determined. Coming on strong is their calling card.

It's pursuit, plain and simple, and a determined one at that.

Harassment? For sure. If the female—who's always the object—stops to peck at a few seeds, she's chased away by the male, who comes up from behind her, being pushy. He walks stiff-legged, flaring his fancy iridescent neck feathers and puffing out his breast to make sure she gets the message. If she's a little slow to cooperate, or stops moving, a swift peck gets her on her way again.

He's protecting his investment in those youngsters to come, driving her away from possible competitors, and back to the nest.

That's the trouble with putting our own spin on the behavior of other creatures.

What seems like the ultimate symbol of romance to us—the sitting side by side, the tender bill touches, the mouth-to-mouth action—falls apart fast when we look at the other totally natural habits of the dove.

Whistle and Clap

> *6 And I said, Oh that I had wings like a dove! for then would I fly away, and be at rest.*
>
> —Psalms 55:6

Doves have remarkable wings. Propelled by the big pectoral (chest) muscles, the birds can fly fast and far. Our North American mourning dove can sustain speeds up to 55 mph, and other species are speed demons, too.

The stiff feathers also make music as doves take to the sky and air passes over and through their pinions.

Often, you'll hear a whistling sound when doves take to the air or come in for a landing, or when a flock passes overhead.

And sometimes you'll even hear a sharp clapping, as the wings slap under the bird's body on takeoff.

Male birds use that clapping flight as a come-on to the female when they're trying to impress during courtship time, but you may also hear the sharp, loud sound of clapping wings when any dove suddenly takes flight.

Going Down

> [16] *And Jesus, when he was baptized, went up straightaway out of the water; and, lo, the heavens were opened unto him, and he saw the Spirit of God descending like a dove, and lighting upon him:*
>
> —Matthew 3:16

Now that would be a sight to see.

One imagines standing awestruck before a pair of elegant, outspread wings and a slow, graceful descent that would wow every watcher on the ground.

Uh…no.

Watch a mourning dove, and you'll see the reality is a little different.

It's often more of an "oh my God!" moment, a sudden appearance rather than a slow descent.

A dove's long, pointed wings give the bird great maneuverability, so it can swerve and dive at high speeds to elude predators that are chasing it in the sky.

Descending is quite the sight too, because doves usually don't glide in from afar to a landing.

Instead, they come in at high speed, then close their wings and drop like rocks, pulling up at the last instant to flutter to a stop, flaring out their tail and throwing it forward to aid in braking.

Whoa! What's *that?!*

> [32] *And John bare record, saying, I saw the Spirit descending*
> *from heaven like a dove, and it abode upon him.*
>
> —John 1:32

I had firsthand experience with the landing method when I raised an orphaned baby pigeon to full maturity.

The bird bonded with me, and seemed to think I was his partner. Often, I'd be walking across a field when I'd spot a far-off dot in the sky, rapidly growing bigger as it approached at 40 mph.

Instinctively, I'd duck my head and pull up my shoulders, as "Pidge" came winging in to land—right on my head—in a great clatter of wings.

After the shock of the sudden landing, Pidge and I greeted each other, he with cooing, me with gentle words. We loved each other, and made sure the other knew it.

> [22] *And the Holy Ghost descended in a bodily shape like a dove*
> *upon him, and a voice came from heaven, which said, Thou art*
> *my beloved Son, in thee I am well pleased.*
>
> —Luke 3:22

Like an Arrow

⁸ Who are these that fly as a cloud, and as the doves to their windows?

—Isaiah 60:8

Once, when I was driving through the farm plains of Texas, a flock of mourning doves rose from a field beside the road and started flying in the same direction my car was heading.

Winging along just a few feet from the shoulder of the road, their flight mirrored my own trajectory.

I was just moseying along that day as usual, taking a little-used back road so I could enjoy the scenery and see whatever there was to see.

With no traffic and good visibility on that long, straight road, I was driving slowly enough to look at plants, birds, or anything else that caught my eye.

The doves passed me like I was standing still.

I glanced down at the speedometer: 30 mph.

Curious to find out how fast they could fly, I hit the gas. Forty, 45, 50, 54—and then I started to outpace them.

I dropped back to 45.

And for two full miles, the "cloud" of doves kept pace with me, flapping along as swift and straight as an arrow.

How long could they have maintained the pace? At least two miles, was what I learned, though the real answer is probably more than that.

After flying alongside me for a couple of miles, the flock suddenly zigged as one and turned away from the road.

Doves of all descriptions make a beeline towards their goal, whether it's a field of grain, a backyard feeder, or a dovecote at the window in old Jerusalem.

Counting Doves

> [6] *And I said, Oh that I had wings like a dove! for then would I*
> *fly away, and be at rest.*
>
>   —Psalms 55:6

By far the most common species in North America are two ubiquitous species that just about everyone is familiar with: the mourning
dove, and the pigeon, more properly called rock pigeon.

Hang on a minute, though—those pigeons, the ones we see
every day in our cities as well as out in the wild, aren't American
birds. Their ancestors were brought along in the very early days of
colonization, and quickly adapted to their new home. They're as
much newcomers to America as any person of European ancestry.

We have another newcomer, too, but this one is a recent immi-
grant: the Eurasian collared dove, who is multiplying fast.

Where'd *You* Come From?

More than 300 different species of doves and pigeons live in various places around the world, making their homes from deserts to tropics to cities and towns.

Some, like our Key West dove, stick to very small areas. Others range far and wide. Perhaps a little too wide, in some cases. We've now got European and Eurasian species making themselves at home in North America.

Keep your eyes open for the large, pale Eurasian collared dove (*Streptopelia decoacta*). It lives in the lands of the Bible, as well as Europe and Asia, and it's spreading fast here. It now nests from Michigan to Montana, south to the Mexican border, as well as along the Atlantic and Gulf coasts.

In some areas, the ringed turtledove (*Streptopelia risoria*) and the spotted dove (*Streptopelia chinensis*)—possibly getting their start when caged birds escaped—are also settling in.

Interestingly, the new birds seem to fit in just fine among our native doves, not causing any problems. Instead, they've found their own niche for food and home sites.

Down in the Valley

> [14] *O my dove, that art in the clefts of the rock, in the secret places of the stairs, let me see thy countenance, let me hear thy voice; for sweet is thy voice, and thy countenance is comely.*
>
> —Song of Solomon 2:14

What's a pigeon and what's a dove? Generally, doves are smaller and svelter than pigeons, with longer tails. But there's another difference, too: the places each chooses to call home.

"Doves of the valley" lived on the plains and deserts of the Bible lands, often around human civilization. And yes, they were mostly doves.

Our American dove species are birds of the valley, too, if by valley you mean just about everywhere near human habitation except in high mountains.

Try to make a valley bird live in the cliffs, and you've got a fish out of water.

It takes doves and pigeons a long time to change their habits, and forcing such a change upon them is a hard thing to ask.

No wonder they were sorrowful at having to leave their home sweet home.

> [16] *But they that escape of them shall escape, and shall be on the mountains like doves of the valleys, all of them mourning, every one for his iniquity.*
>
> —Ezekiel 7:16

Pigeons were—and are—the main species that nested on cliffs in the wild. Instead of building a platform of sticks on the limb of a tree or among the supporting branches of a bush or even right on the ground, in the case of some species of the Middle East, they tuck their homes into holes and on sheltered ledges on the rocky face of the cliff.

> [28] *O ye that dwell in Moab, leave the cities, and dwell in the rock, and be like the dove that maketh her nest in the sides of the hole's mouth.*
>
> —Jeremiah 48:28

Today, our city pigeons often substitute a ledge of a building or a bridge as a nesting site.

They nest in colonies, which can cause problems for city-dwellers who have to walk through the collected droppings, feathers, and other debris beneath the ledge.

Not all pigeons live in cities, though.

Some of those we call rock pigeons have kept their wilder habits. Ornithologists differentiate them from city birds, calling them "feral pigeons."

You can still see these pigeons nesting on cliffs all across America, winging their way across the canyon or chasm. Next time you visit the Grand Canyon, keep your eyes open for pigeons perched or flying near their homes on the biggest cliff of all. And listen for the echo of their flapping wings as they rocket out from the cliffs.

Not a Mean Bone in Their Bodies

> [16] Behold, I send you forth as sheep in the midst of wolves: be ye therefore wise as serpents, and harmless as doves.
>
> —Matthew 10:16

In Matthew's account, Jesus introduces his disciples by name, and sends them out into the world with guidelines on how to behave.

The dove was a fitting symbol for a standard of behavior that was to be completely unconfrontational.

Or, perhaps, gentle but clever.

Whichever dove we're looking at, one thing is immediately clear: These are the baby lambs of the bird world.

They're sweet and gentle, and rarely if ever resort to confrontation, let alone outright fighting.

> [19] O deliver not the soul of thy turtledove unto the multitude of the wicked: forget not the congregation of thy poor for ever.
>
> —Psalms 74:19

Keep your gentle turtledove soul, urged the Psalmist. Other birds may stab at each other or batter with wings, but you—well, don't engage. Stay sweet.

When push comes to shove, doves would rather flee than fight.

Even when two male doves are competing over a female, they resort at most to flaring their wings and tail and making a mild threatening gesture with their not-very-scary little bills.

Flight or Fight?

[11] Ephraim is also like a silly dove without heart: they call to Egypt, they go to Assyria.

—Hosea 7:11

That Ephraim! Although the second son of Joseph, and a tribal patriarch of Israel, he has "mixed himself among the people," sharing their sinful ways: he is "a cake not turned" (Hosea 7:8).

Yep, he's half-baked, that Ephraim, because although he started out on the right path, he has forgotten to worship God and, instead, like the rest of his people, has gotten mixed up with the pleasures of Baal.

At the time of God's scolding, it's courage that is called for in Ephraim. Courage to get in gear and lead his people back to the ways God intended.

Being likened to a dove—well, God did not intend it as a compliment in this case. Doves are well known for flight, not fight: They rarely stand up to a threat, preferring instead to flee.

[12] When they shall go, I will spread my net upon them; I will bring them down as the fowls of the heaven; I will chastise them, as their congregation hath heard.

—Hosea 7:12

Go ahead, says God, fly hither and yon like a dove. No matter how you fly, I'll still find you.

¹¹ They shall tremble as a bird out of Egypt, and as a dove out of the land of Assyria: and I will place them in their houses, saith the Lord.

—Hosea 11:11

Along with other prophets, Hosea took on the job of reminding the Israelites that they had strayed—and that there were going to be consequences.

This was their last warning. It was way past time to get back on the straight and narrow, before God laid waste to the kingdom.

But they needed to move, and move now.

Time for the Exodus—led by Moses into Egypt. Ahead lay sanctuary, and a return to God's good graces, eventually.

But the journey would not be undertaken without fear and trembling, noted Hosea—quivering like the bird of Egypt, and the dove of Assyria.

Which dove?

Likely, that of the famed "voice of the turtle"—either the (Eurasian) turtledove or its similar relatives.

In fall, doves from all over Europe retreat to their winter homes in "Assyria"—what is now northern Iraq—down into Egypt and southward.

Come spring, doves that wintered in Africa fly north by the millions, into and through Palestine and Israel and other modern countries of the lands of the Bible.

Some stay in their Middle East breeding grounds, while the rest spread out throughout Europe, all the way up into Scandinavia, and eastward into Russia and Mongolia.

Every fall, the cycle repeats itself.

Hither and yon. Hither and yon.

Say "Aww"

What is it about miniature versions of familiar animals that makes us melt? Little dogs have been favorites of royalty and the rest of us for ages, starting with the Pekingese and pugs of ancient Chinese dynasties, the Japanese chin given as a gift to the Empress in the eighth century, and the Maltese terrier of the Mediterranean, once known as the "Roman ladies' dog."

Miniature horses, dwarf goats, tiny rabbits—downsized animals have their loyal fans, no matter what the species.

Now, how about a dove that's only as big as a sparrow? Go ahead, everybody say "Aww...."

It's the Namaqua dove—a tiny dove that's only 8 inches long, with roughly half of that length being its long tail.

It's a common species of near-desert wild places of the Middle East, and like all its other cousins, it says coo. Or, to transcribe that mournful call more exactly, *hoo-hoo kuh-whooo.*

Squab for Supper

> [25] *Ye shall therefore put difference between clean beasts and unclean, and between unclean fowls and clean: and ye shall not make your souls abominable by beast, or by fowl, or by any manner of living thing that creepeth on the ground, which I have separated from you as unclean.*
>
> —Leviticus 20:25

An abundant food source is a real treasure, whether it's leftover grain in a farm field—or the big flocks of doves gathered to eat that grain. And humans are just as opportunistic as any other animal on the face of the earth.

Doves aren't on the very specific list of "unclean" birds that are so carefully delineated by name in the books of Deuteronomy and Leviticus.

So, by default, their tasty meat falls on the okay-to-eat side of God's law.

And eaten, they were.

With all those dove species in the Middle East, it's no surprise that doves went onto the plate—or off the roasting spit and straight down the hatch, before the use of plates.

Domesticating doves so that food was ready anytime you wanted it got its start in the Middle East, too, say historians.

Many homes had their own dovecote attached, where a few of the rapidly reproducing birds could be grabbed for dinner anytime. Cheap protein, and tasty, too!

Young birds, about a month in age, were the prime target of diners, because their meat was more succulent than the tougher flesh of their parents.

Tastes like chicken, say fans of the delicacy. Dark-meat chicken, tender and juicy.

'Til Death Us Do Part

[11] Of all clean birds ye shall eat.

—Deuteronomy 14:11

Numbering around 350 million strong, the gentle—and tasty—mourning dove is one of the most abundant species in America.

About 20 million mourning doves may fall to the gun in a given year, but that barely makes a dent in the thriving population.

Even with all those hunters taking to the fields, the mourning doves manage to maintain their numbers just fine, thank you.

But why doesn't that population of doves increase by leaps and bounds?

If one pair can produce as many as 20 young'uns in a year, multiplied by, let's say, 100 million or so breeding pairs—well, you'd think we'd be kicking our way through a solid sea of doves every time we step outside to walk to the other side of the yard.

Ah, it's not easy being a dove—mourning, turtle, or any other species, including pigeons.

Every predator around enjoys a fine meal of dove or squab, as the youngsters are called. Snakes raid the nests. Foxes, coyotes, wandering cats, and other four-footed predators pounce on birds on the ground or raid nests.

Danger from the sky can come home to roost, too. Falcons and hawks pick the birds right out of the air, or dive on them when they're foraging in fields. Owls may prey on their nests at night, snatching adults or babies alike.

And cars take a toll, as well, when doves fly low across a road.

No need to worry about organizing a Golden Anniversary party for your pair of devoted doves.

What's the wedding anniversary gift for brief milestones—paper? Yep, that's more like it.

Sad to say, a wild dove's life often lasts only a single year.

A Shameful Slaughter

One flock—*one flock!*—of passenger pigeons in Ohio, reported in 1866, was a mile wide and 300 miles long.

An estimated 3.5 billion birds, which took 14 hours to pass a specific point.

Cheap food—for slaves, for pigs, and for the poor in crowded cities as well as countryside.

And unimaginably easy to harvest, since the birds flew, roosted, nested, and fed in those immense flocks.

At first, the decline was slow, almost barely noticeable. But as the forests on which the birds depended for food—beechnuts and acorns were their main menu—were cleared, the rate accelerated.

Then, rail lines were installed across America. That was the final straw for the now-extinct passenger pigeon. Although the birds had been hunted ever since man appeared, it was open season big-time once the rail lines went in.

Millions upon millions of these tasty birds were caught in nets—thousands at one throw—or shot, or whacked with sticks, or intoxicated with alcohol-soaked grain, so they could be packed in barrels and shipped via rail to New York, Boston, and other places.

Their natural habit of living communally hastened their demise.

These birds nested in huge colonies that covered many square miles—850 square miles in one site in Wisconsin—with hundreds of nests in each tree. They traveled to feeding places and salt licks in unimaginable numbers. All-too-easy targets, for the market hunters who lay in wait at the pigeons' usual haunts.

By 1914—barely 50 years after that giant Ohio flock was noted—the species was down to one lonely bird, Martha, who lived out the last of her days at the Cincinnati Zoo.

I like to think she was dreaming of eating beechnuts, surrounded by her many friends, there at the end.

A New Leaf

> [11] *And the dove came in to him in the evening; and, lo, in her*
> *mouth was an olive leaf pluckt off: so Noah knew that the*
> *waters were abated from off the earth.*
>
> —Genesis 8:11

Finally, we get to the most famous dove of all: Noah's dove.

We already know the Biblical significance for celebrating this dove's behavior: "Yay, we're saved!"

But could there be a biological reason behind the dove bringing back a sprig of greenery?

You bet!

Birds pluck leaves for two reasons: To tuck into their nests, or to eat.

None of the 300 or so dove and pigeon species worldwide use leaves in their nests. Sparrows do. Purple martins do. Red-shouldered and red-tailed hawks do.

Perhaps as a deterrent to parasites. Perhaps to humidify the eggshells. Perhaps—well, nobody really knows.

What we do know, though, is that doves don't do it. No fresh greenery in the nest.

Food for Thought

Many birds—from big plump grouse to little house finches—eagerly nibble leaves or buds. But I've never seen an American mourning dove nor a rock pigeon chomping on the greenery.

Scientists concur, noting that our North American doves eat almost entirely seeds, augmented by a bite of fruit on occasion for some species.

But doves of other places are a little different.

The Bible lands see a lot of different doves and pigeons. Some only pass through at migration time, but others nest and live there.

Since the Bible doesn't tell us which species Noah had aboard, we can only speculate as to the identity of the dove who brought back such glad tidings.

But detective work is fun!

And in this case, digging deep into the natural history behind the Bible leads us to the identity of the only possible species among all those two-by-two birds and animals on the Ark.

Narrowing It Down

Grain and seeds are the main diet of the resident Mideast birds, just as they are of our American species.

Some species eat only seeds, so we can cross those off the list of possibilities right away.

Other species of faraway lands, including the fabulous, bright-colored "fruit doves" of the Tropics, eat a lot of, yep, you guessed it, fruit.

But greenery? We're still hard-pressed to find doves that deign to eat leaves.

Out of the 300 or so worldwide species, only a handful of doves in the area of the Bible occasionally add a bit of "salad" to their main diet of seeds.

- The **Oriental turtledove** (*Streptopelia decaocto*) eats "tips of grass shoots and occasionally other greenstuff." (Quoted food habits are from the book *Doves and Pigeons of the World,* by Derek Goodwin.)

- The (Eurasian or European) **turtledove** (*Streptopelia turtur*) eats "leaves of sainfoin and probably other leaves and buds." (Sainfoin is *Onobrychis viciifolia,* a legume that also grows wild in North America.)

- The **stock pigeon** (*Columba oenas*) occasionally eats "young buds, shoots, and leaves." But mainly, like the others, it eats seeds.

Yep, could be any of those three. Maybe.
But wait.
There's another species that's an even better possibility.
The most likely suspect?
The **wood pigeon** (*Columba palumbus*).

Ta-Da!

The lovely wood pigeon looks a lot like our rock pigeon, but with extra flash—a pretty white patch on its neck, a boldly striped tail, and showy white splashes in its opened wings.

We don't have wood pigeons in North America. But it's a common bird in Bible lands, as well as throughout Europe and Britain.

And, according to British Museum of Natural History expert

Derek Goodwin, the wood pigeon "has a very varied diet including flowers and young leaves of many plants...."

Not just "occasionally," you'll notice. Nope, these doves—which would've been very familiar to people at the time of the Bible—enjoy a leafy, flowery salad as a regular thing.

Aha! Got'm!

Now, why did the dove bring back the olive leaf instead of just eating it himself?

A Gift of Love

> [9] *But the dove found no rest for the sole of her foot, and she returned unto him into the ark, for the waters were on the face of the whole earth: then he put forth his hand, and took her, and pulled her in unto him into the ark.*
>
> —Genesis 8:9

Even before the olive-leaf dove, Noah had made an earlier try with a dove. Still too much water. No place to perch.

So she returned, until sent out the second time, when she plucked the olive leaf.

The scenario makes perfect sense.

But, "she"?

Many folks refer to any dove as "she." Maybe it's that gentle quality, which seems to lean towards the feminine side rather than the macho.

At any rate, the Bible refers to Noah's dove as a female.

I don't think so.

As we've seen, the pair bond between a couple of doves is incredibly strong. The birds are true to one another, and the partnership is forged for life. Even if that life is brief.

One of the tender gestures with which birds cement that pair bond is by feeding each other.

The behavior is known as *courtship feeding,* and it takes place both before nesting and while the female is incubating her eggs.

Nearly always, it's the male who offers the female a special morsel, selected just for her.

So, if Noah's dove was actually a male, and only called "she" because of the inherent gentleness of the birds, then the dove's return with a young, tender olive leaf makes perfect sense, biologically speaking.

That released dove who'd managed to find an olive tree above water was returning to the Ark with a special treat for his mate.

After eating who-knows-what for many days on board, a bit of fresh greenery would be a real treasure to a wood pigeon.

Yum! An olive leaf! Thanks, partner!

Gone but Not Forgotten

> [12] *And he stayed yet other seven days; and sent forth the dove; which returned not again unto him any more.*
>
> —Genesis 8:12

Male doves and pigeons are the ones who establish the nesting territory. The male bird claims an area and begins defending its boundaries even before he establishes a partnership with a female.

Since that dove's mate was still captive on the Ark, the newly free bird was probably getting busy at setting up a home.

> [19] *And of every living thing of all flesh, two of every sort shalt thou bring into the ark, to keep them alive with thee; they shall be male and female.*
>
> —Genesis 6:19

All other life had been destroyed in the great Flood, so the stakes were even higher for both members of the dove couple. Only one pair of these doves—er, wood pigeons—in the whole world.

The male dove who didn't return to the Ark had more important matters on his mind. He was making sure everything would be in order for his partner, with a home ready and waiting when it was nesting time.

Bought & Sold

> [12] *And Jesus went into the temple of God, and cast out all them that sold and bought in the temple, and overthrew the tables of the moneychangers, and the seats of them that sold doves,*
>
> [13] *And said unto them, It is written, My house shall be called the house of prayer; but ye have made it a den of thieves.*
>
> —Matthew 21:12-13

It was a busy time for the merchants near and in Herod's Temple. Hundreds of thousands of pilgrims had come to Jerusalem for Passover, and a brisk trade was being done in exchanging various currencies for Tyrian money.

Jews weren't allowed to mint their own money, so the procedure was a necessary part of the pilgrimage for many.

The Court of the Gentiles, inside the Temple but apart from areas of worship, was one big bazaar.

Vendors offered trinkets and food, and animals were on hand, too, ready for purchase once a pilgrim's money had been changed into the coin of the realm.

Uh-oh. Big mistake. Because one of those on hand was Jesus, along with his disciples Matthew, Mark, Luke, and John.

No mixing commerce and prayer, and the Temple was dedicated to the worship of God.

Time to clean up your act, moneychangers and dove sellers!

Perhaps Jesus had been frustrated by the situation for quite a while, although this is the first time we hear of it. At any rate, he went ballistic. The account of Jesus and the moneychangers is the only time in the Bible that he resorts to physical violence. All four of the Gospels agree, telling the same story of Jesus throwing tables over and making a scourge, a whip, to chase the mercenary folks right out.

> [15] *And they come to Jerusalem: and Jesus went into the temple, and began to cast out them that sold and bought in the temple, and overthrew the tables of the moneychangers, and the seats of them that sold doves;*
>
> —Mark 11:15

No word on what happened to those doves they were selling, but it's nice to think that they flew safely away.

After all, they weren't on the overturned tables—those belonged to the moneychangers. The birds, perhaps tethered, more likely in cages, must've been sitting beside the seats of the dove sellers.

As to why doves were being sold, that leads us to two possibilities: as food, or as sacrifices.

Food is a possible selling point. Maybe they were already cooked and being sold as ready-to-eat snacks? Possible.

But more probable is that they were intended as sacrifices. Now, *there* was a ready market.

> [14] *And found in the temple those that sold oxen and sheep and doves, and the changers of money sitting:*
>
> —John 2:14

Oxen and sheep? They're not supper on the hoof, but sacrificial animals available for sale to anyone who needed to make the ritual.

Doves? Just a smaller, more convenient, and no doubt cheaper version.

Doves to Spare

> *29 And on the eighth day she shall take unto her two turtles, or two young pigeons, and bring them unto the priest, to the door of the tabernacle of the congregation.*

> —Leviticus 15:29

Doves get the biggest number of shout-outs in the Bible—about 50 references in the Scriptures, either to doves or to the larger pigeons.

Some of those lines pertain to the gentle personality of these birds, making us smile because we, too, love their dark eyes, their quiet nature, their endearing habit of living near humans and being easy to tame.

Some of the mentions to doves in the Bible are in reference to their voice, or to their swift flight, or to their habits of nesting in valleys or on cliffs.

But many of the Biblical references have a darker side.

Let's start with a look at those dove sellers at the Temple—the ones that aroused Jesus's ire.

It may seem barbaric to us nowadays, but sacrificing animals to God was a big part of the ancient tradition. Rituals were spelled out in detail in the Bible, and doves often featured prominently.

There were plenty of them, and thanks to their trusting nature, they were easy to net or nab.

Here's the how-to of the sacrifice ritual, spelled out in Leviticus, describing the necessary steps to heal a leper:

> *4 Then shall the priest command to take for him that is to be cleansed two birds alive and clean, and cedar wood, and scarlet, and hyssop*

> *5 And the priest shall command that one of the birds be killed in an earthen vessel over running water:*

> *6 As for the living bird, he shall take it, and the cedar wood, and the scarlet, and the hyssop, and shall dip them and the living*

> *bird in the blood of the bird that was killed over the running*
> *water:*
>
> *⁷ And he shall sprinkle upon him that is to be cleansed from the*
> *leprosy seven times, and shall pronounce him clean, and shall*
> *let the living bird loose into the open field.*
>
> —Leviticus 14:4-7

Further exhortations to sacrifice a dove or a pair of them (as well as other animals) are scattered throughout the Old Testament, starting with Genesis.

The circumstances under which such a sacrifice was recommended may change, but the general purpose is always the same: Someone had transgressed, and the sacrifice was a way to make things right with God again, to atone for bad behavior.

I'm not so sure the doves were okay with that.

The how-to sure is graphic, but that wouldn't have been distasteful to anyone who raised, hunted, or bought live doves to use as food.

> *¹⁵ And the priest shall bring it to the altar, and wring off his*
> *head, and burn it on the altar; and the blood thereof shall be*
> *wrung out the side of the altar:*
>
> *¹⁷ˢ And he shall cleave it with the wings thereof, but shall not*
> *divide it asunder: and the priest shall burn it upon the altar,*
> *upon the wood that is upon the fire: it is a burnt sacrifice, an*
> *offering made by fire, of a sweet savour unto the Lord.*
>
> —Leviticus 1:15, 17

Good thing there were a lot of doves in the Bible lands, because sacrificing them was commonplace in those days.

The priests known as Levites, who wrote the Book of Leviticus in the Bible (some believe Moses wrote this book, but many scholars believe otherwise), laid out the rules and rituals for both the priesthood and the laity.

Many possible occasions for sacrificing doves are mentioned, in Leviticus 5:7, 12:6, 12:8, 14:22, 14:30, 15:14, 15:29, as well as in Numbers 6:10.

Only one mention of sacrificing doves shows up in the New Testament, in the Gospel of Luke, after the birth of Jesus.

Mary, Joseph, and their newborn are heading to Jerusalem, planning to observe a traditional ritual:

> [24] *And to offer a sacrifice according to that which is said in the law of the Lord, A pair of turtledoves, or two young pigeons.*
>
> —Luke 2:24

That's the last sacrifice of doves mentioned in the Bible. Why? The ritual was no longer necessary.

> [28] *Verily I say unto you, all sins shall be forgiven…*
>
> —Mark 3:28

> [3] *For I delivered unto you first of all that which I also received, how that Christ died for our sins according to the scriptures:*
>
> —1 Corinthians 15:3

Cutting a Covenant

> *⁹ And he said unto him, Take me an heifer of three years old, and*
> *a she goat of three years old, and a ram of three years old, and*
> *a turtledove, and a young pigeon.*
>
> —Genesis 15:9

The initial instructions from God, about the animal sacrifice Abraham (Abram) needed to make, are nice and clear:

Heifer? Check. She goat? Check. Ram? Got it. Turtledove? Pigeon? Ready when you are.

But then things get murky. Or, at least, hard to imagine, if one isn't familiar with the ways in which binding deals were made in Bible days.

> *¹⁰ And he said unto him all these, and divided them in the midst,*
> *and laid each piece one against another: but the birds divided*
> *he not.*
>
> —Genesis 15:10

In other words, Abraham cut all of the animals in half, except for the dove and pigeon, and separated them into two piles.

Why? Because that's how you do the first step when you "cut a covenant," which is the old-time Mideast turn of phrase for sealing a deal. In Hebrew, the verb used in the phrase "making a covenant" is *krt*, "to cut." And that cut is meant literally. The language may also be the source of today's expression, "cutting a deal."

When the parties to the agreement walked between the two piles of halved animals, the deal was sealed.

In the case of Abraham, when the sun went down that night, God made his pass-through in the form of a burning lamp.

A warning may have also been implicit in the symbolism of beasts cut in half: Renege on this deal, and you may end up like these animals.

Covenants are to be kept. Especially those made with God.

When Israel broke the deal and turned to worship of Baal, God reminded the people that that major slip wasn't something he would take lightly.

Destruction of Jerusalem by the Babylonian army was coming, warned Jeremiah the Prophet, reporting God's words:

> *18 And I will give the men that have transgressed my covenant, which have not performed the words of the covenant which they had made before me, when they cut the calf in twain, and passed between the parts thereof,*
>
> *19 The princes of Judah, and the princes of Jerusalem, the eunuchs, and the priests, and all the people of the land, which passed between the parts of the calf;*
>
> *20 I will even give them into the hand of their enemies, and into the hand of them that seek their life: and their dead bodies shall be for meat unto the fowls of the heaven, and to the beasts of the earth.*
>
> —Jeremiah 34:18-20

Food of Last Resort

> *25 And there was a great famine in Samaria: and, behold, they besieged it, until an ass's head was sold for fourscore pieces of silver, and the fourth part of a cab of dove's dung for five pieces of silver.*
>
> —2 Kings 6:25

We already know that doves aren't on the "Do Not Eat" list in Deuteronomy and Leviticus.

So we can scarf them down with a clear conscience. And with, um, relish.

But dove droppings?

Most birds carry their nestlings' droppings away from the nest, letting them fall from their bill at some distance from home. Doves and pigeons aren't as tidy. They allow the droppings to accumulate, perhaps because they help reinforce the nest as they dry and harden.

Eating other animals' dung isn't unheard of. The droppings may still hold some value as nourishment, because not all food gets fully digested as it passes through.

Even though the lumps on that nest would peel off in tidy chunks ("cabs"), it would have to be as a food of last resort. Especially at that inflated price of "five pieces of silver."

Think I'll take a bite of that donkey's ear instead, thanks. Hey, maybe it'll taste like chicken.

DOVE

Mourning dove (*Zenaida macroura*),
Rock pigeon (*Columba livia*),
and other species

American range: Mourning dove and rock pigeon, abundant across the entire country; Eurasian collared dove, spreading fast; other species, limited in range.

Natural diet: Seeds, grain, occasionally fruit or berries.

At the feeder: Millet, milo, cracked corn, bread.

American species: Native: mourning dove, white-winged dove, Key West quail-dove, Inca dove, ruddy ground dove, common ground-dove, band-tailed pigeon, white-tipped dove, white-crowned pigeon, red-billed pigeon. Introduced: Eurasian collared dove, ringed turtledove or Barbary dove, spotted dove, rock pigeon.

Species in the Bible area: (Eurasian or European) turtledove, Oriental turtledove, palm turtledove, Eurasian collared dove, African collared dove, rock pigeon, stock pigeon, wood pigeon, many others.

A note on translation: In Hebrew, the turtledove is *tôr;* again, a word that echoes what the bird says. Other doves fall under the Hebrew word *yônah.*

Chapter 12

Sparrow

Even the Least

⁶ *Are not five sparrows sold for two farthings, and not one of them is forgotten before God?*

—Luke 12:6

I have a soft spot for the underdog. And that includes the house sparrow.

Also known as the English sparrow, this little chirpy bird is despised in America by many—dare I say "most"?—people.

And beloved by others, including me. And God, according to the Bible.

When I moved to southern Indiana, I learned the house sparrow goes by another name in some areas.

Spatzie.

A name that lends itself nicely to the scornful tone usually used when these birds are mentioned.

As in, "How do I get rid of these spatzies at my feeder?"

A softer variation, *spotsie,* is used near Chicago and in some other regions.

Both come from the German word *Spatz,* which simply means "sparrow."

But with its nasal A and fricative Z, which lend themselves so nicely to spitting the word out with disgust, *spatzie* is way more fun to say.

And if you find yourself becoming fond of the birds, you can change that Z to a gentler S, and call them *spatsies.* Which makes the birds sound cute, rather than reviled.

Old World or New World?

House sparrows are Old World sparrows.

They aren't related, except very distantly, to our New World sparrows.

Not close kin to our white-throated sparrow.

Nor to our song sparrow.

Nor to our white-crowned, golden-crowned, field, tree, chipping, grasshopper, Savannah, or any other of the dozens of other native American species.

The word "sparrows" in this verse of the Bible is a translation of the Hebrew transliteration *sipporim.*

Which means "sparrows."

Ah, but *which* sparrows?

Some scholars say the word means "any little birds."

I'm inclined to think it means "any sparrows," of which there were probably a billion birds, of several very similar species, at the time the Bible was written.

Why sparrows?

Because the sound of the Hebrew word for one sparrow—*sippowr,* or its varying transliterated spellings—sounds just like the sound of a little sparrow chipping.

Little Chippies

> *14 They, and every beast after his kind, and all the cattle after their kind, and every creeping thing that creepeth upon the earth after his kind, and every fowl after his kind, every bird of every sort.*
>
> —Genesis 7:14

The sparrows of the Bible hark back to a Hebrew word, which is transliterated into the English alphabet as *sippowr*. Or *tsipowr, tsippor, tzippor, tsipor, tzipor, sipporim,* or *çippôr*, depending upon which origin you're looking at.

Go ahead, say it out loud, repeating it rapidly.

Sounds a lot like a sparrow chipping, doesn't it?

All of those words are onomatopoetic—they spell out a sound phonetically. And the definition is "one who makes that sound," that is, one who chirps or twitters.

The writers of the King James Version weren't very consistent in their translation of that word.

Sometimes it's translated as "sparrow." Sometimes it becomes just plain old "bird."

In this Bible version, another word stood in for birds in general: *hā·'ō·wp̄,* which usually became "fowl," meaning, "Yeah, some kind of bird or birds we aren't going to bother to name." Not what we think of today as fowl, that is, chickens or turkeys or other yummy things for our plate. But just a generic bird.

"Every fowl after his kind" means a whole multitude of different kinds of fowls, or birds.

But then, in the same verse, we come to *"every bird of every sort."*

In the Hebrew, that word is *sippowr*. A twittering sparrow.

And now the passage makes sense: We've got birds of every kind, and, among them, sparrows of every sort.

Little Brown Lookalikes

At first glance, all sparrows look alike. They're small. They're brown.

And they're so notoriously hard to identify that many bird-watchers lump them all together as LBJs—"little brown jobs."

Sure, each species has its own distinguishing characteristics, whether it's a head cap of a certain color, an eye stripe, a streaky breast, or other distinctions.

But those are pretty subtle differences, and they require a close look at the bird to pinpoint it.

And sparrows—our native New World species, that is—are skulkers.

They usually stay low to the ground, or hide within weedy patches or the brushy edges of woods, fields, and roadsides.

Seems they know they're low birds on the food chain—easy pickings for hawks and other predators, should they come out in the open. Which is why many birdwatchers take one glance at that bunch of little birds that refuse to leave the brush, and give up on trying to sort them out. LBJs, good enough.

In the lands of the Bible, sparrows aren't nearly as reclusive.

Old World sparrows are often out in the open, living among people. Still, they're tricky to separate, because they're lookalikes—they all look very much like our familiar house sparrow.

So the Hebrew word *sippowr* might refer to any or all of these birds, all of them super-abundant in Bible lands:

- **House sparrow** (*Passer domesticus*)
- **Dead Sea sparrow** (*Passer moabiticus*)
- **Spanish or willow sparrow** (*Passer hispaniolensis*)
- **Eurasian tree sparrow** (*Passer montanus*), another species introduced to North America and thriving in St. Louis.

Most of these species winter in Africa; some, in the Bible lands themselves. The long-distance travelers pass through in multitudes of millions during migration, funneling through to Africa.

Won't You Be My Neighbor?

Passer domesticus

—Scientific name of the house or English sparrow

The Latin word *Passer* simply means "sparrow." But see that word *domesticus*? That sums it up. These little brown guys are domestic.

They like to live near people. Very near people.

As in, right in the walls or eaves of our houses, or in any other nook or cranny they can stuff with grass, straw, and all sorts of other debris that looks like good building material to their eye.

You won't find house sparrows out in the middle of nowhere, no matter what the terrain.

Not in deep forests. Not on high mountaintops. Not in open plains. Not among the cactus of the desert. No rocky cliffs, thanks.

These chirpy guys want to be our neighbors.

So they're common in cities, in towns, around farms, and at bird feeders and trash dumpsters just about everywhere.

Even the Least of These

> ²⁹*Are not two sparrows sold for a farthing? and one of them
> shall not fall on the ground without your Father.*
>
> —Matthew 10:29

> ⁶ *Are not five sparrows sold for two farthings, and not one of
> them is forgotten before God?*
>
> —Luke 12:6

Buy four, get a fifth sparrow free? What a bargain!

But not likely that anyone in Bible lands at the time these verses were written would have had a farthing in their pocket.

That's a British coin, worth a quarter of a penny.

Still, it gets the point across.

Whether we're paying with farthings, or with the currency of the time, sparrows are cheap. So cheap, that they were a popular substitute for more expensive doves, when poor people needed birds to make a sacrifice.

Yet, even though these birds were worth practically nothing in terms of money, the disciples Matthew and Luke pointedly remind us in these verses that they were just as important to God as the biggest, grandest eagle.

Nobody escapes notice.

Including those practically worthless sparrows.

What's in Your Pocket?

Roman coins were the currency of the time.

The currency was the only accepted payment for the tax collected in Jerusalem. And they were the only payment accepted by merchants, including those who sold sparrows.

Those moneychangers in the Temple? They were changing the

currency of other places into the acceptable Roman, or Tyrian (from the city of Tyre), coins.

Various coins changed hands, including the *assarion,* or *as,* and its less valuable fractions, from the *semuncia* (1/24 the value) to the *semi* (1/2 the value), to the *bes* (2/3 the value).

In some Bible translations, the word *assarion* is used instead of "farthing" in the verses from Matthew and Luke about the value of a sparrow or two or five.

A whole assarion or a fraction thereof?

That's unclear, but it doesn't much matter. Like the farthing, none of these coins carried much value.

The Color of Money

As long as we're talking about money, and Tyrian items, how about one of the earliest status symbols?

In the days of the Byzantine Roman Empire, only the wealthy and royalty were able to wear the color purple.

Not just any purple, though.

Nope. What the high-class folks wanted was "Tyrian purple," a saturated reddish-purple hue.

Regular old purple notoriously faded in the strong sun of the Mideast. But Tyrian purple got even stronger and brighter the longer the garment was exposed to sun.

"Purple for dyes fetched its weight in silver," noted the ancient historian Theopompus. And "a certain woman named Lydia, a seller of purple" is told of in the Bible, in Acts 14:16.

The source of this status symbol? A little less than glorious.

Tyrian purple, named for the city of Tyre on the Mediterranean Sea, was made from mucus. Slimy, squished snail bodies. The "spiny dye-murex" sea snail (*Bolinus brandaris*) was responsible for those envious glances.

His Eye Is on the Sparrow

His eye is on the sparrow, and I know He watches me.

—Civilla Martin, with credit to Mrs. Doolittle

Although it's one of the best known Bible references, this line actually never appears in the Bible.

Its impetus certainly does, in the words of the disciples Luke 12:6 and Matthew 10:29 we read earlier.

But the language is from a popular hymn, called, naturally, "His Eye Is on the Sparrow."

Written in 1905, the lyrics were inspired by a remark by the wife of an elderly, infirm couple, Mr. and Mrs. Doolittle of Elmira, New York.

Despite their physical ailments and difficulties, the Doolittles somehow always remained cheerful, and in good spirits.

How did they manage to stay focused on the positive, always smiling instead of complaining about their lot in life?

Civilla Martin, who was visiting the couple along with her husband, the Rev. Walter Martin, asked what their secret was.

"His eye is on the sparrow, and I know He watches me," replied Mrs. Doolittle.

Civilla, who'd written many hymns with her husband, recognized a great line when she heard it.

According to her letters, in which she recounted the incident (although she never did mention the first names of the couple, as far as I could tell), she grabbed her notebook and turned that line into an uplifting poem, right there on the spot.

She and her husband, the Rev. Martin, had collaborated on many hymns, with him composing the music for her words.

But for this one, it wasn't Civilla's husband who set Mrs. Doolittle's words (and Civilla's poem) to music. It was the Rev. Charles Gabriel (nice name, eh?), another prodigious composer of hymns, who came up with the music for this classic.

And classic it is. Dozens of artists have recorded the song— from Ethel Waters, Mahalia Jackson, and Andy Griffith, to name a few. More recently, Jessica Simpson, Crystal Lewis, and Whitney Houston have added their voices to Civilla's hymn of hope.

A Loving Heart

[31] *Fear ye not therefore, ye are of more value than many sparrows.*

—Matthew 10:31

Following close on the heels of his words about the El Cheapo sparrows sold in the old markets—the birds that God watches, even though they were worth barely a penny—Matthew makes another point in this verse:

If God knows when one of those little birds fall, surely He keeps his eye on people, too.

Immigrants by Invitation

House sparrows aren't American birds by origin, although they sure have made themselves at home here.

In the smoky cities of nineteenth-century America, birds were absent.

Our native birds were accustomed to clean air and countryside, and they didn't move into the cities that were springing up.

And city folk missed them.

In 1851, the Brooklyn Institute of Arts and Sciences (now the Brooklyn Museum) decided to do something about the situation.

According to the 1889 recollections of the Institute's Nicolas Pike (which are in dispute by some historians), the institution bought 100 pairs of house sparrows from England, for the grand sum of $200—and grand it was: that'd be about $6,000 today, way more than two-for-a-farthing—and released them.

Eight pairs were set free in New York City, followed by two larger releases. Undigested oats in the horse manure that littered the streets is credited as the food that sustained the birds.

Twenty years later, more were released, in San Francisco and Salt Lake City.

We all know the end of this story.

Today, house sparrows flourish in just about every town and city across America. Even without horse manure.

Years ago, I was doing a breeding-bird count for the Audubon Society when I spotted an active purple martin colony in the yard of a small farmhouse in the flatlands of Indiana.

Pulling a few feet into the driveway to count the pairs of martins swooping over and around their apartments, I couldn't help but notice small wire cages on the ground near the base of the pole.

Several of the cages—which were actually traps—held frantic

house sparrows. A few of the birds sat dejectedly in the cages, but most fluttered desperately against the bars.

House sparrows originated in the Middle East, where many of them make their homes in the gigantic nests of storks and herons.

When the sparrows spread to Europe and Great Britain, they adopted nesting places in ivy-covered walls, in the nests of magpies, and anywhere else they could find a sheltered niche.

In America, house sparrows took up cavity-nesting in a big way, using holes in dead trees and any birdhouse they could squeeze into, as well as the eaves of houses or any enclosed space they could find—barns, warehouses, factories.

House sparrows are gregarious by nature, hanging out in chattering bunches and nesting in close proximity to each other when circumstances allow.

Purple martin houses, with their inviting array of side-by-side compartments, are an irresistible attraction to a happy bunch of the little brown birds.

As for the caretakers of those martin houses, saying they're not big fans of house sparrows is putting it mildly.

"What's the story with the sparrows?" I asked, when the homeowner approached, bracing myself for the answer.

"God will forgive me," he answered with a smile, making a neck-wrenching motion with his hands.

" 'His eye is on the sparrow,' " I said simply, taking my leave.

That's not a quote from the Bible. But it *is* based on the sentiment in those pages—even the smallest living thing is worthy of notice, and of love.

He noticed those sparrows fall.

Fear not, as Matthew and Luke wrote reassuringly.

In or Out?

"The sparrow hath found an house," says the Psalmist in 84:3.

What sort of house? That depends.

House sparrows are highly adaptable birds. In the wild, they nest in natural holes—in banks or trees—or in the branches of trees. But when there's a human-made cavity available, they move right in.

Birdhouses are fair game, and they're often the most desirable real estate as far as sparrows are concerned.

But the little chirping birds will happily adopt a crack in your house siding or hole in the eaves, or a wall densely covered in ivy or other vines.

Soffits—the covered eaves just below the roof—are a top target. Sparrows will find any crack or hole in that area and wiggle their way inside.

No Need to Go It Alone

> [7] *I watch, and am as a sparrow alone upon the house top.*
>
> —Psalms 102:7

The Psalmist was sad and lonely in this chapter, recounting his woes and lamenting about his sense of isolation.

So he chose a strong symbol. A single sparrow.

House sparrows, and the other Old World sparrows in the lands of the Bible, do not go it alone.

Only once have I seen a house sparrow sitting by itself.

Its mate had been killed that morning by a roaming cat.

The male sparrow was alone on the rooftop. My rooftop, where he and she used to sit, happily chirping.

Now he was quiet.

He was mourning.

Within days, though, the male bird had moved on. He'd partnered with another female, and they were working on a nest.

Easy Come, Easy Go

House sparrow life is like one big singles' bar. Always plenty of extras to go around, should one of a pair lose its partner.

And sparrows aren't shy about public displays of affection. They don't care who's watching when they mate.

In fact, they're so randy that they've been a symbol of sex since people first took notice, thousands of years ago.

Chaucer invoked the sparrow in his description of the Summoner character in his prologue to *The Canterbury Tales*: "As hot he was, and lecherous, as a sparrow."

The male house sparrow is the more, um, uninhibited, shall we say. Which did not escape the Greek philosopher Aristotle.

"Females live longer than males if the males are salacious," wrote Aristotle. "Accordingly cock-sparrows have a shorter life than the females."

Shakespeare's *Measure for Measure* features a judge who refuses to recognize a marriage, even though the couple is living together as man and wife. That clears the way for the husband to be executed for committing fornication.

"Sparrows must not build in his house-eaves," sarcastically says the husband's friend Lucio, speaking of the judge, "because they are lecherous."

And *Culpeper's Complete Herbal* (1652) recommended eating the birds as an aphrodisiac, noting, "the brain of sparrows when eaten provokes the lust exceedingly."

Nesting Needs

*³ Yea, the sparrow hath found an house, and the swallow a nest
for herself, where she may lay her young, even thine altars, O
Lord of hosts, my King, and my God.*

—Psalms 84:3

House sparrow nests are not very tidy, to say the least.

In fact, they're downright messy.

When the birds make their home in a nest box, you know
who's the occupant from a long way away. How? Because pieces of
string and grass and strips of paper and plastic will be dangling
out the door.

That gives sparrow-despisers even more ammunition for their
scorn towards these little birds.

Not only did the house sparrows evict the bluebirds who
wanted that box—the bluebirds you dearly wanted—the sparrows
aren't even good housekeepers.

As a messy housekeeper myself, I'm on the sparrows' side.

But there's an even better reason to give them a pass on their
untidy habits: It's just natural behavior for these birds.

House sparrows are "true sparrows," according to those who decide such things. They belong to the Passeridae Family.

Our 20-some native species of American sparrows are not "true sparrows." They belong to the Emberizidae Family. We call them sparrows, but in other parts of the world, they're called buntings.

So we can't expect house sparrows to behave like our shy song sparrow, or to make a neat little nest like our chipping sparrow.

Since we're already accustomed to calling our native birds "sparrows," here's an easier way to sort it out:

Our native birds are *New World sparrows*. The house sparrow and other species of the Bible lands are *Old World sparrows*.

Kissing cousins? Not by a mile. These birds aren't even in the same family.

Down Go the Dominos, Bang Goes the Gun

One poor house sparrow met its demise in 2005, when it accidentally toppled 23,000 dominos in one fell swoop.

The dominos were just a small part of the 4 million pieces set up to try to beat a world record. Luckily, gaps had been left in place until the last minute, to prevent all of the millions of pieces from falling, should someone accidentally make a false move.

But the organizers of the event, the Dutch TV production company Endemol, hadn't factored in a klutzy sparrow. And they weren't about to take any further chances. They hired a pest control company to get rid of the bird.

When trapping failed, it was "So long, sparrow," as a gunshot rang out. Which sort of ruined the festive atmosphere for a lot of people. Animal-rights organizations got involved, and publicity was a little less than positive. As in, death threats to the TV and pest control companies.

But the sparrow was immortalized. Known as the "Domino Day Sparrow," it was stuffed and displayed in a Dutch museum.

Beware of Wiles

^{16} I have decked my bed with coverings of tapestry, with carved works, with fine linen of Egypt.

^{17} I have perfumed my bed with myrrh, aloes, and cinnamon.

^{18} Come, let us take our fill of love until the morning: let us solace ourselves with loves.

^{19} For the goodman is not at home, he is gone a long journey:

^{20} He hath taken a bag of money with him, and will come home at the day appointed.

^{21} With her much fair speech she caused him to yield, with the flattering of her lips she forced him.

^{22} He goeth after her straightway, as an ox goeth to the slaughter, or as a fool to the correction of the stocks;

^{23} Till a dart strike through his liver; as a bird hasteth to the snare, and knoweth not that it is for his life.

—Proverbs 7:16-23

Trickery is the name of the game when it comes to catching a man, according to this chapter of Proverbs (and the similar Proverbs 6).

Note the warning signs, say the verses, spelling out the whole bag of tricks, from smiling lips to "Hey, Handsome, my husband's out of town...."

Get out while you can, is the point of Proverbs, instead of falling prey to the wiles of a wicked woman.

Looking beneath the oh-so-tempting surface is never a bad idea.

Neither is pausing to consider the consequences of a moment's pleasure.

Yet, when temptation beckons, even our human brains have difficulty remembering those concepts.

And when it comes to sparrows, well, those little brown birds don't have notably big brains.

Spread some grain in your trap, and all sparrows can think is, "Food! Oh boy, food!"

The entire flock alights to feast on the grain, not knowing it was spread by a hunter lying in wait.

Too bad they didn't realize beforehand that it was going to be their last supper.

Worse yet, even after the trap is sprung and the birds collected, the hunter can do it again in just minutes. The rest of the flock just don't learn their lesson, it seems. (Ravens are a lot brighter at figuring out a trap, as you can read about in Chapter 4.)

Which bird is the target of those snares in Proverbs 7:23? According to the transliterated Hebrew, we're talking sparrows here (*sippowr*).

Hunting sparrows was a normal part of life for people in the Old World. Even today, the practice continues, despite being outlawed in many countries.

There are just too many tempting feathered morsels flying around. And sparrow pie is mighty tasty. Or so I've heard.

Catching the birds was a cinch. House sparrows and Eurasian tree sparrows are gregarious birds that travel, feed, and roost in companionable flocks.

One quick cast of the net, and you might have a dozen for supper, with leftovers for breakfast.

Flee for Your Life!

> [7] *Our soul is escaped as a bird out of the snare of the fowlers: the snare is broken, and we are escaped.*
>
> —Psalms 124:7

Sparrow snares, or traps, might've been set on the ground. Either a single net or a pair of nets, ready to yank upon the birds after they alighted, were utilized.

Snottygobbles

Poor birdies—land on a twig, and suddenly you can't move, other than to frantically flap your wings. Your feet are glued in place.

What did the glue come from?

Berries or bark from the Syrian plum tree; some members of the holly family; mistletoe; or parts of a few other plants.

Including sebestens, the berries of flowers and trees of the *Cordia* genus of the Old World.

Otherwise known as—ready?—snottygobbles.

They didn't go by that name in Bible times, but it sure is descriptive. The berries of *Cordia,* used for birdlime in Damascus during Bible times, are thick with mucus. (In western Australia, a different plant is also called snottygobbles, for the same reason.)

Traps were baited with grain. Something that sparrows find way more alluring than a flirtatious woman.

But sometimes, the bird managed to escape.

Broken fibers in the net, an incomplete throw, a bad aim, a sudden leavetaking by the flock—any misstep in the hunting technique, and the birds flee.

But if the snare was a nefarious sticky trap, not a net, well, the chances of an escape were mighty slim.

Coating twigs and branches with an adhesive was a popular method for snaring small birds.

Sad to say, it still is, even in countries such as Italy and Malta where this traditional "hunting" method is now illegal. Even as recently as 2013, the practice was still going on.

Known as birdlime, the once-popular bird trap is an adhesive made by boiling certain parts of various plants, fermenting the liquid, then adding oil.

After the plant stuff is thickened in the pot, the glue is painted onto twigs, ready to snag any bird that lands there.

Sorry, sparrows, you poor guys have "hasteth to the snare," and never saw the trap awaiting you.

And that mistake, as Proverbs 7:23 warned, will cost your life.

I Wonder as I Wander

> [8] *As a bird that wandereth from her nest, so is a man that wandereth from his place.*
>
> — Proverbs 27:8

Like the hundreds of other pithy one-liners in Proverbs, this verse is meant to stand on its own.

Apparently, in the view of the writer (who may have been the wise King Solomon), wandering from home is not a good thing.

If that man who "wandereth from his place" is a man with family, then no, the urge to move on alone is definitely not a good thing.

In today's world, though, folks relocate all the time, pulling up roots for better opportunities or even better climate. Yep, the grass is always greener. And the kids get scooped right up to move, too.

Not so with birds.

Although the general range of many species is shifting northward in response to climate change, after they've built their nest, they're going nowhere.

All birds are bonded to their nest. Wander? No way.

A nest holding eggs or babies is the culmination of lots of work, and the birds' main reason for being.

The King James translators went with "bird" again this verse, instead of "sparrow," which the Hebrew *sippowr* seems to call for.

Fine.

All birds, sparrows among them, are strongly connected to their home and babies. Well, wait, there are a couple of exceptions—cowbirds and European cuckoos deposit their eggs in other species' nests and fly away, dusting their hands of the duties of childcare.

But for other birds, if the nest happens to be destroyed—by wind, weather, predators, or people knocking that messy thing down from the eaves—the birds rebuild.

And rebuild.

And rebuild.

The dedicated couple keeps try-try-trying again until the time gets too short to successfully raise a bunch of babies and get them on their own before winter sets in.

Down the Hatch

> [18] Now that which was prepared for me daily was one ox and six choice sheep; also fowls were prepared for me, and once in ten days store of all sorts of wine: yet for all this required not I the bread of the governor, because the bondage was heavy upon this people.
>
> —Nehemiah 5:18

Yes, it's sparrows again (*sipporim*), translated in the King James Version as "fowls" this time.

Although all manner of little birds went down the hatch, sparrows were probably the most commonly eaten, simply because there were way more of them than of other birds.

Sparrows have been eagerly eaten by humans for thousands of years.

They're not on the "do not eat" lists that are spelled out, bird by bird, in the books of Leviticus and Deuteronomy.

And with such an abundant source of protein, ripe for the plucking, who's not going to take advantage of them?

Even today, sparrows still go onto the plate in many places.

Here's part of a letter to the London *Sunday Times* in 2003:

"In a Middle Eastern restaurant recently the owner proffered one of the house specialities [sic], a plate of roasted sparrows. I tried to eat one, daintily plucking the legs off—but my host showed me the way by popping a whole one into his mouth and crunching with a satisfied grin."

Uh, no, thanks, I'm stuffed, can't eat another bite.

Sparrow pie was once a popular dish in England, when "sparrow clubs" flourished. Their purpose being to go out and catch sparrows, of course, and even compete at pubs to see who got the most.

You could start a sparrow club yourself in the U.S. today, if you were so inclined. For house sparrows, that is. Although our native New World sparrows are protected by federal law, house sparrows are not, because they're a non-native species.

Oh boy! Eat 'em up!

Need a recipe?

You can find directions for "How to Cook Sparrows" online. Seems the little birds have caught the attention of at least some survivalist-type folks.

Bon appetit!

French Accent

In France, it's the ortolan (*Emberiza hortulana*) that goes crunch-crunch on those sophisticated palates.

When it still has its feathers, the ortolan looks a lot like the house sparrow: a little streaky brown bird.

When it's prepared for eating, the bird looks like a tiny naked chicken. A sad bite or two, swimming in sauce.

That "preparation," by the way, means plucking the feathers. Every other bit—bones, beak, innards—is left intact.

Not even the finest French sauce could entice me to take a bite.

But the French feel differently. Ortolan is what French president François Mitterand requested for one of his final meals, when he neared the end of his days.

Following the traditional protocol, he draped a cloth over his head while he munched away on the delicacy.

And ortolan is what Craig Claiborne, famed food critic of the *New York Times,* wanted to eat, when he won a fine meal in France at a charity auction.

Killing ortolans has been banned since 1999, but there's still an illegal trade in the birds.

Plenty of ortolans probably went down the hatch in the time of the Bible, too, because these sparrow-lookalikes migrate in force across that area when they're going to and from their winter home in Africa.

An Ear on the Sparrow

Scene: St. Helen's Church in Brant Broughton, Lincolnshire, a lovely 13th century stone church with soaring spires. August, 1979.

The audience was in their seats.

The recital by famed classical guitarist Konrad Rogossnig was about to begin.

Recording engineers were at their controls, ready to capture the concert for the BBC.

And a house sparrow was chirping.

And chirping.

And chirping.

It just would not shut up.

So the pastor of the church, the Rev. Robin Clark, had the bird shot.

The reviews of the event? Overwhelmingly negative, no matter how sublime the music may have been.

Unceasing Slaughter

[52] Mine enemies chased me sore, like a bird, without cause.

—Lamentations 3:52

Ah, the importance of a comma! That little punctuation mark connects the sparrow (translated "bird" in the King James Version, but originating in that word *sipporw*) to the "sore chase" in this verse. Not to "without cause."

Cause is easy to determine, in the case of sparrows.

They were the focus of the hunters' chase as food or as a source of income—to be sold in the marketplace for snacks or for sacrifices (for the cheap price of two-for-a-farthing, or a portion of an assarion). Catch enough sparrows, and that little bit of money would add up.

The chase of sparrow-hunters wasn't a chase in the literal sense, of course, because most of the time was spent in hiding, waiting to yank the net.

No mistake, though, sparrows were sorely beset.

And still are today.

Many sparrows are now protected by law. But in some countries, no such restrictions exist. Even in America, the house sparrow is fair game.

Besides, there's still poaching to satisfy that appetite.

Countryfolk in Europe and other places are accustomed to eating sparrows and other small birds. The tiny fowls are a traditional dish, and I imagine they're even more welcome in times of economic troubles, such as occurred recently.

But if bird-eaters are reluctant to flout even a loosely enforced law, why, there's still smuggling to fill the gap and fit the appetite.

In 1993, close to 2 million plucked and frozen Eurasian tree sparrows bound for Italy were confiscated; in 2007, another 2 million were nabbed coming in from China.

Sudden Decline

The urban decline did not become obvious until about 1990,
where in the centres of some large towns the decline, unlike
that in farmland, took place at an increasing rate leading to
virtual extinction.

—J. Denis Summers-Smith,
"Changes in the House Sparrow Population of Britain"

Imagine if all the house sparrows you love to hate suddenly disappeared.

All the house sparrows at your feeder.

All the house sparrows in town, squabbling over trash in the gutters or crusts in the park.

All the sparrows hanging out in fast-food parking lots.

It'd be a different world.

And it already is in London, Edinburgh, Hamburg, Paris, and other European cities, where the house sparrow population has crashed dramatically, beginning in the late 1970s.

The birds everyone took for granted in Europe's cities are vanishing. And fast.

And no one knows why.

The expert-of-experts on house sparrows, J. Denis Summers-Smith, was just as baffled as everyone else was, when the problem first came to light.

"One of the most remarkable wildlife mysteries in the last 50 years," he said in an interview, as clueless as anyone who puts out crumbs in the backyard for their usual batch of sparrows.

By 2002, the house sparrow made its first appearance on the International Union for Conservation of Nature (IUCN)'s Red List of species of conservation concern.

The species had met one of the dismal criteria for inclusion—its worldwide numbers had declined by more than 50% in the last 25 years.

Oh no! What in the world was going on?

Starving to Death?

A British newspaper, *The Independent*, put up a £5,000 prize in 2000, to anyone who could explain what had happened to the sparrows.

The prize is still unclaimed, although a group of researchers, led by Kate Vincent of De Montfort University in Leicester, offered an explanation in 2008, after studying the problem.

It was bugs, they said. Not enough insects.

Nestlings starved to death.

Why no bugs?

Could be the common use of pesticides in home gardens, which annihilated zillions of aphids, spiders, beetles, and other critters that the birds depend upon.

Or it could be the widespread use of agricultural chemicals, including neonicotinoids (restricted in Europe beginning in December, 2013), which reduce the insect population in farm fields to practically zilch.

Or it could be shifts in insect populations because of climate change, an effect that's already being documented around the world.

When insects hatch at the wrong time—a week or two earlier or later—their peak is no longer timed to the needs of nesting birds in the area.

We still don't know the answer for sure, although lack of insects seems to be the direction most research is heading.

As of 2013, the prize is still up for grabs. And house sparrows are still declining.

Going Down

The global population of house sparrows seems too big to fail. More than 540 million breeding pairs, estimates the International Union for Conservation of Nature (IUCN), which tracks species numbers around the world.

"Despite the fact that the population trend appears to be decreasing," says the IUCN's 2013 fact sheet, "the decline is not believed to be sufficiently rapid to approach the thresholds for Vulnerable under the population trend criterion (>30% decline over ten years or three generations)."

That's the global picture.

Country by country, the story is way gloomier.

In the United Kingdom alone, house sparrows declined by 65% from 1977 to 2000.

For some reason, it seems to be worst in U.K. cities (almost total collapse), very bad in suburbs (60% decline), and bad, but not quite so dire (48%), in rural areas, according to a survey by the British Trust for Ornithology.

Other countries of Europe are reporting similar scenarios.

In North America, we haven't seen a decline. Yet.

See that noisy bunch out there at the feeder? The little brown guys gobbling up all your seeds and scraps and even those pricey mealworms?

Count yourself lucky.

And let's all keep our eye on the sparrow.

HOUSE SPARROW
(*Passer domesticus*)

American range: Ubiquitous in towns, cities, suburbs, farms, and around any other human habitation, from sea to shining sea.

At the feeder: Millet, cracked corn, bread, baked goods, and if those are absent, just about any seeds or scraps.

American species: Although we have dozens of native New World sparrow species, the house sparrow and, in very limited areas, the Eurasian tree sparrow are our only Old World sparrows.

Species in the Bible area: House sparrow, same as ours; plus related lookalikes (Dead Sea sparrow, Spanish sparrow, Eurasian tree sparrow).

A note on translation: The Hebrew transliteration of "sparrow" is spelled differently in various sources: *sipporim, tsippor, tzippor,* and other variations. Translators differed on the interpretation of the word; you can read more about the issue earlier in this chapter.

Bibliography

The *King James Version* of the Bible, *Strong's Exhaustive Concordance*, the *Septuagint,* and the *Masoretic Text* were consulted frequently in the writing of this book.

Three online sources were also invaluable:
* *For Scripture quotes:* www.biblegateway.com
* *For translations from the transliterated Hebrew:* www.biblos.com
* *For bird biology:* "Birds of North America Online," Cornell University Lab of Ornithology, www.bna.birds.cornell.edu/bna/

In addition to the sources cited above, these publications provided detailed research and information referred to in this book:

Abramson, L. 2013. "Israel Restores Wetlands; Birds Make It Their Winter Home." National Public Radio (NPR); February 24, 2013.

Anderson, H. C. 1909. *Tales.* Harvard Classics, Volume 17.

Aristotle. 350 B.C.E.; reprinted 2011. *On Longevity and Shortness of Life.* Boston: Charles River Editors, e-book, 2011.

Audubon, J. J. 1840. *The Birds of America.* New York and Philadelphia: Audubon and J.B. Chevalier: 1840.

Axelson, Gustave. 2012. "Dinner Guests: Common Ravens may be why wolves hunt in packs." *Living Bird* magazine, Cornell University, Spring 2012.

Bagglioni, V., Canestrari, D., Chiarati, E., Vera, R., Marcos, J. 2010. "Lazy group members are substitute helpers in carrion crows." *Proceedings of the Royal Society for Biological Sciences,* 2010.

Bang, B. G. and S. Cobb. 1968. "The size of the olfactory bulb in 108 species of birds." *Auk* 85:55-61.

Barrows, W. 1889. "The English Sparrow (*Passer domesticus*) in North America, Especially in its Relations to Agriculture." United States Department of Agriculture, Division of Economic Ornithology and Mammalology Bulletin. Washington: U.S. Government Printing Office.

Bent, A.C. 1919-1968. *Life Histories of North American Birds.* 21 volumes. Washington: U.S. Government Printing Office, 1919-1968.

Boarman, W. and Heinrich. B. 1999. "Common Raven (*Corvus corax*)." In *The Birds of North America,* No. 476 (Poole, A., ed.). The Birds of North America Online, Ithaca, New York.

British Trust for Ornithology (BTO). 2012. "BTO Garden BirdWatch survey, House Sparrow numbers 2003-2012."

Bureau of Land Management (BLM). 2008. "Decision Record and Finding of No Significant Impact for the Environmental Assessment Predatory Animal Damage Control on public lands Sweetwater, Lincoln, Uinta, and Sublette Counties." Rock Springs BLM District Office: Rock Springs, Wyoming.

Chaucer, G. Circa 1470; reprinted 2004, Olson, G. and Kolve, V., eds. *The Canterbury Tales.* New York: W.W. Norton & Co., 2004.

Collopy, M. W., and Edwards, T.C., Jr. 1989. "Territory size, activity budget, and role of undulating flight in nesting Golden Eagles." *Journal of Field Ornithology* 60:43-51.

De Laet, J., and Summers-Smith, J.D. 2007. "The status of the urban house sparrow *Passer domesticus* in north-western Europe: a review." *Journal of Ornithology,* 148 (2, supplement): 275-278.

Easton, A., and Emery, N., eds. 2005. *The Cognitive Neuroscience of Social Behaviour.* Oxford, UK: Psychology Press, 2005.

Eaton, M. 2005. "Human vision fails to distinguish widespread sexual dichromatism among sexually 'monochromatic' birds." *Proceedings of the National Academy of Sciences of the United States of America* (PNAS) 102 (31).

Ekman, J. and Ericson, P.G. 2006. "Out of Gondwanaland; the evolutionary history of cooperative breeding and social behaviour among crows, magpies, jays and allies." *Proceedings of the Royal Society: Biological Sciences* 273 (1590): 1117-25.

Ekman, J. 2013. Faculty page, Population Biology, Evolutionary Biology Centre, Uppsala University, Uppsala, Sweden. Online at www.ebc.uu.se/Research/IEG/zooeko/People/Jan_Ekman

England, Little Johnny. 2009. "Welcome to the Sparrow Club." (Song, from the album *Tournament of Shadows.*) Kent, UK: Talking Elephant, 2009.

Eraud, C., Dorie, A., Jacquet, A. and Faivre, B. 2008. "The crop milk: a potential new route for carotenoid-mediated parental effects." *Journal of Avian Biology* 39 (2): 247–251.

Franzen, J. 2010. "Songbirds poached and eaten." *The Telegraph*, November 8, 2010.

Goodwin, Derek. 1983. *Doves and Pigeons of the World.* Ithaca, New York: Cornell University Press, 1983.

Graczyk, M. 2012. "Texas vulture study upends forensics." The Associated Press, March 8, 2012.

Hart, B. 1990. "Behavioral adaptations to pathogens and parasites: Five strategies." *Neuroscience & Biobehavioral Reviews* 14(3):273–294.

Hasselquist, D. and Sherman, P. 2001. "Social mating systems and extrapair fertilizations in passerine birds." *Behavioral Ecology* 12 (4): 457-466.

Heinrich, B. 1999. *Mind of the Raven: Investigations and Adventures with Wolf-Birds.* New York: Ecco, 1999.

International Union for Conservation of Nature (IUCN). 2013. "Species factsheet: *Coturnix coturnix.*" BirdLife International. Online only, www.iucnredlist.org/details/100600195/0

International Union for Conservation of Nature (IUCN). 2013. "Species factsheet: *Passer domesticus.*" BirdLife International. Online only, www.iucnredlist.org/details/106008367/0

Johnston, R. F. 1992. "Rock Dove," in *The Birds of North America*, No. 13. Academy of Natural Science and American Ornithologists' Union, Philadelphia, PA.

Jones, M., Pierce, K., Jr., Ward, D. 2007. "Avian vision: a review of form and function with special consideration to birds of prey." *Journal of Exotic Pet Medicine* 16 (2): 69–87.

Kalmbach, E. R. 1939. "American vultures and the toxin of clostridium botulinum." *Journal of the American Veterinary Medical Association* 94:187-191.

Lepage, Denis. "Checklist of Birds of Israel." *Bird Checklists of the World.* Avibase. Online only, at www.avibase.bsc-eoc.org

McCarthy, M. 2000. "It was once a common or garden bird. Now it's not common or in your garden. Why?" *The Independent,* May 16, 2000.

McCarthy, M. 2008. "Mystery of the vanishing sparrow." *The Independent,* November 20, 2008.

McCarthy, M. 2010. "Mystery of the vanishing sparrows still baffles scientists 10 years on." *The Independent,* August 19, 2010.

Moulton, M., Cropper, W., Jr., Avery, M., and Moulton, L. 2010. "The Earliest House Sparrow Introductions to North America." USDA National Wildlife Research Center, Staff Publications, Paper 961.

O'Harra, D. "Ravens in the City." *Far North Science,* Anchorage, AK; online only, no date. www.farnorthscience.com/cold-quests/ravens-in-the-city/

Ohishi, I., Sakaguchi, G., Riemann, H,. Behymer, D., and Hurvell, B. 1979. "Antibodies to Clostridium botulinum toxins in free-living birds and mammals." *Journal of Wildlife Diseases* 15 (1): 3-9.

Phillips, R. L. 1986. "Current issues concerning the management of Golden Eagles in western U.S.A." Pages 149-156 in Birds of Prey Bulletin no. 3. (Chancellor, R. and Meyburg, B., Eds.) World Working Group on Birds of Prey and Owls, Berlin, Germany.

Pliny (author) and Rackham, H. (translator). 1938. *Pliny: Natural History.* Cambridge: Harvard University Press, Loeb Classical Library, 1938.

Seibt, U. and Wickler, W. 1978. "Marabou Storks Wash Dung Beetles." *Zeitschrift für Tierpsychologie* 46 (3): 324–327

Shakespeare, W. 1601; reprinted 2004, 2006. "The Phoenix and the Turtle." Reprinted in *Shakespeare's Sonnets and Poems* (Mowat, B. and Werstine, P., eds.), Washington, D.C.: Folger Shakespeare Library, 2004, 2006.

Shakespeare, W. 1603; reprinted 2005, Mowat, B. and Werstine, P., eds. *Measure for Measure.* Washington, D.C.: Folger Shakespeare Library, 2005.

Shaw, L.M., Chamberlain, D., Conway, G. and Toms, M. 2011. "Spatial distribution and habitat preferences of the House Sparrow *Passer domesticus* in urbanized landscapes." British Trust for Ornithology (BTO) Research Report 599.

Silver, Rae. 1984. "Prolactin and Parenting in the Pigeon Family." *The Journal of Experimental Zoology* 232 (3): 617–625.

Steudler, P.A., and Peterson, B.J. 1984. "Contribution of gaseous sulphur from salt marshes to the global sulphur cycle." *Nature* 311: 455-457.

Stevenson, H. M. 1974. "Florida region." *American Birds* 28: 628-632.

Stevenson, H. M. 1978. "Florida region." *American Birds* 32: 339-342.

Stott, John. 2003. In "Stop the Week: Winner's Letters." London *Times,* January 26, 2003.

Summers-Smith, J. D. 1992. *In Search of Sparrows.* London: T. & A. D. Poyser, 1992.

Summers-Smith, J. D. 2005. "Changes in the house sparrow population in Britain." International Studies on Sparrows 30: 23–37.

Summers-Smith, J. D. 2009. "Family Passeridae (Old World Sparrows)." In del Hoyo, J., Elliott, A., David, C., *Handbook of the Birds of the World. Volume 14: Bush-shrikes to Old World Sparrows.* Barcelona: Lynx Edicions, 2009.

Swope, W. 2011. "How to Cook Sparrows." Online only, at www.livestrong.com/article/486894-how-to-cook-sparrows/

Trail, P.W. 2005. "What is 'Marabou'?" *Identification Guides for Wildlife Law Enforcement* No. 8. U.S. Fish & Wildlife Service, National Fish and Wildlife Forensics Laboratory, Ashland, OR.

Troscianko, J. 2012. "Binocular bird's eye view something for corvids to crow about." (Video.) Reuters. Online at www.uk.reuters.com/video/2012/12/31/binocular-birds-eye-view-something-for-c?videoId=240210070

U.S. Geological Survey (USGS). 2011. "Thumbs Up or Down to Annual Burning of a Tidal Marsh in Maryland?" *Fire Science Brief,* Issue 134, May, 2011.

United Press International (UPI). 1979. "Disturbing chirps get bird shot at church." UPI London; *Modesto Bee,* August 9, 1979.

Vergara, P. and Aguirre, J. 2006. "Age and breeding success related to nest position in a White Stork *Ciconia ciconia* colony." *Acta Oecologica* 30 (3): 414-418.

Vergarra, P. and Aguirre, J. 2006. "Nest-site fidelity and breeding success in White Stork *Ciconia ciconia*." *Ibis, International Journal of Avian Science* 148 (4): 672–677.

Wackenhut, M. 2009. "Management of American White Pelicans in Idaho. A Five-year Plan (2009–2013) to Balance American White Pelican and Native Cutthroat Trout Conservation Needs and Manage Impacts to Recreational Fisheries in Southeast Idaho." Idaho Department of Fish & Game, August 17, 2009.

Ward, J., McCafferty, D., Houston, D., and Ruxton, G. 2008. "Why do vultures have bald heads? The role of postural adjustment and bare skin areas in thermoregulation." *Journal of Thermal Biology* 33 (3): 168–173.

Wimberger, P. 1984. "The Use of Green Plant Material in Bird Nests to Avoid Ectoparasites." *Auk* 101 (3): 615-618.

Winsor, D., Bloebaum, P. and Mathewson, J. 1981. "Gram-negative, aerobic, enteric pathogens among microflora of wild Turkey Vultures (*Cathartes aura*) in west central Texas." *Applied Environmental Microbiology* 42: 1123-1124.

Zuckerbrot, Y.D., Safriel, U., and Paz, U. 1980. "Autumn migration of quail *Coturnix coturnix* at the North Coast of the Sinai Peninsula." *Ibis, International Journal of Avian Science* 122 (1): 1–14.

Index

Illustrations

Cast & Crew

Heather Dieter Bartmann

Heather was born in England and grew up in then-rural Naperville, Illinois. She graduated from the American Academy of Art in Chicago and studied ornithology at Colorado State University. She maintains her studio near the foothills in Fort Collins, Colorado, painting the birds of Colorado and their habitat with the enthusiasm and awareness that comes from years of close study.

Often choosing the less spectacular, seldom painted species, Heather captures bits of their day to day lives, private moments often unseen by the casual passerby. Her work has won national awards and been featured in magazines and galleries. See more of her beautiful paintings and prints at www.heatherbartmann.com.

Lou Bartmann

Raised in the suburbs of Chicago, Lou attended the Ray-Vogue School of Photography and the American Academy of Art. After working several years for the prestigious B. C. Kassell Company, an engrossing and illuminating studio in Chicago's Loop district, Lou and his family moved to

a remote canyon in the mountains of northern Colorado.

Now retired and living in Fort Collins with his wife Lila, Lou continues to appreciate and capture birds and other wildlife with his camera. He also does special lettering projects from time to time under the influence of persuasive family members and friends.

Behind-the-Scenes Support: *Dixie, Koko, and 02*

Dixie the border collie and her sidekick Koko love walks in the woods (as long as there's a stick involved), sunsets (which means it's close to dinnertime), and daisies (great for digging up). But their favorite thing of all is playing "get the stick" for hours at the Oregon coast or any other large body of water. After which the car and sleeping bags are never the same.

02 (pronounced "Oh Two"; it's a serial number: 01 is no longer among us) is a 15-pound Genuine Buckhorn Supercat. Although of the feline persuasion, 02 is a fierce guard dog who drives off coyotes, bears, moose, and any visiting dogs he happens to dislike. Which is most of them.

Sally Roth & Matt Bartmann

Sally's an award-winning author of 20 or so popular books about birds, nature, and gardening, and a contributing editor for *Birds & Blooms*. She's also an enthusiastic public speaker, whether it's grabbing a stranger on the street ("Hey, want to see something cool?") or talking to an audience of hundreds ("Hey, want to see something cool?"). Matt, who missed being a native Coloradoan by just a year or so, is a photographer and old Volvo fixer-upper and has been putting words to paper since age 6, when he wrote and illustrated his epic 10-page biography, *Sam the Dog*.

But mostly we're just a couple of nuts who somehow managed to find each other and have been having fun ever since. We don't call ourselves writers: We're naturalists. We love nature. And learning. And laughing. And life.

Come visit us at www.sallyroth.com. We'd love to see you!

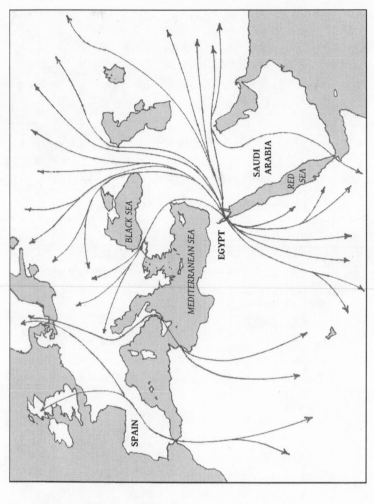

General Migration Routes

At bird migration time, the lands of the Bible are like the waist of a gigantic hourglass.

Millions upon millions of birds pour down from Europe and Asia, traveling towards Africa. Most of them cross over the "bridge" of the Bible lands. .

The incredible spectacle repeats itself every spring and fall, as great eagles, vultures, falcons, cranes, storks, and hundreds of other species make the awe-inspiring journey towards home.

Made in the USA
San Bernardino, CA
19 January 2014